# WINTERSET IN TIME
## GROWING UP GAY IN SMALL TOWN IOWA

Phillip Truckenbrod

*A HollyGrove Book*

Copyright © 2020 Phillip Truckenbrod
For reprint or extensive quotation permission please email
phil.truckenbrod@gmail.com
with the text involved and a description of proposed use.
Short quotations may be used without written permission if author and book credits are given in the resulting text.

Cover Photo by Teddi Yaeger

teddiyaeger.com

(Madison County Courthouse, Winterset, Iowa)

Also by this author

## "Organists and Me:
## Half a Century as an Agent for Musicians"

Available from Amazon.com

"*Organists and Me*, by legendary impresario Phillip Truckenbrod, is a deeply personal, candid, and literate memoir that should be read by performers and by those who work in the arts."

–Anthony Baglivi, Editor Emeritus, *The American Organist*

*for John*

# Contents

Preface .................................................................................................. i
1) January A Love Affair With Snow ................................................ 1
   Supervising Officer ........................................................................ 3
   Into The Arms Of Teachers ........................................................... 5
2) February Unisex Valentines ........................................................ 6
   Pragmatic Romance ...................................................................... 7
3) March My Life With Words ....................................................... 11
   Double Dating As A Trio .............................................................. 13
   Trying To Be Just One Of The Boys ............................................. 17
4) April Marshmallow 'Cheeps' & Jelly Beans ............................... 20
5) May Baskets of Violets ............................................................... 25
6) June The Birds & The Bees ....................................................... 30
7) July Parades, Fireworks & Picnics ............................................ 37
8) August Fair Time ....................................................................... 44
9) September Sleep-Overs ............................................................. 52
   Sex Ed, Winterset Style ................................................................ 57
10) October The Odor of Burning Leaves ...................................... 62
    The Adults' Favorite Holiday ..................................................... 67
11) November The Family at Table, Including Our Crazy Uncle ....... 69
    The 'hired man' Moves In .......................................................... 74
12) December Tinsel That Hangs Straight .................................... 78
13) Sunday The Lord Shares His Day With The Open Road ......... 84
14) Monday Wild Flowers For A Tame Boy .................................. 91
    Another Side To The Coin .......................................................... 93
15) Tuesday More Words ............................................................... 97

Additional Sex Ed, Winterset Style .................................................. 98
16) Wednesday Highways Through the Centers of Towns ............ 103
    Germany, Britain, Iowa ............................................................ 106
17) Thursday Beware Yellow Unless it Flies ................................... 111
    Birds Of A Daring Yellow .......................................................... 112
18) Friday Like The Other Boys ....................................................... 115
19) Saturday On The Town ............................................................. 119
20) Leap Year Bonus Day ............................................................... 123
    Cusp Of A New Era .................................................................. 131
21) Every Season Of The Year Be Nice ......................................... 134
    One Threatening Gray Cloud On The Horizon ....................... 138
22) A Town for All Seasons ............................................................ 140
    A Boyhood Paradise ................................................................ 143
    Winterset The Secure .............................................................. 150
    Penney's On The Square ......................................................... 155
    West, Toward Denver .............................................................. 158
Postscript 1: Acquiring an Adjective In A Place Like Winterset ...... 162
Postscript 2: On Losing My Brother, A Winterset Fixture ............... 168
Postscript 3: The Small Town As An American Icon ....................... 177

# Preface

When I think of Winterset the sun comes out.

Sure, childhood had its bloody knees and bruised egos, its betrayals and dashed hopes. Kids struggled through puberty. People got sick. People were poor. People died. But at least everything except early television was in beautiful, vibrant, living color. Color so determined that it pierced the rainiest day. Color that illuminated even where light had difficulty penetrating.

And one did not have to be a Pollyanna to see the color. It was free to all. It rested on the foundations of greetings that actually seemed to spring from the heart, of honesty, earnestness, good will and faithful striving. It was the Boy Scouts, and church, and the first violets of spring all rolled into one pallet of vivid, reassuring color. It was the color of…well, it was the color of home.

No, Winterset wasn't all sweetness and light—it was a real place, inhabited by real people who were subject to influences and circumstances they could not always control. But the other side of that coin was that almost everyone tried to be nice to each other and seemed to genuinely hope that things were going well for the other guy. Niceness was a civic duty and a civic habit, as I'll try to explain to you later. This made life in Winterset, for lack of a better word, "nice" for the most part. For a child, at least, it sparkled in the clear light of day.

Of course, I was seeing Winterset through the eyes of a child so there may have been a lot of rough edges which didn't register with me fully. And the adults obviously had to shoulder concerns which hadn't dawned on me yet.

But I'm sure this pleasant and picturesque little town harbored no more ill-will than the minimum required by the laws of nature. Everyone, at very least, tried to be pleasant and caring even when they might be themselves hurting on the inside. It might not have been a dictate of nature that we should be nice to each other, but if so no one had told the population of Winterset.

One of the hallmarks of small town life is that everyone knows everyone else, and for that matter almost everything *about* everyone else. And, admittedly, sometimes folks probably *knew* things about each other which were not actually true at all. This could be annoying or frustrating; there were few secrets successfully kept, or at least kept for very long.

But it could also be a blessing in disguise. People tend not to hate people they know, or maybe even just people whom they *think* they know.

# Preface

So knowing each other built up a layer of insulation against nastiness, and to a large extent against even simple indifference. Everyone was a neighbor, even if some neighbors lived closer-by than others. One hopes for the best when it comes to neighbors because one is part of the neighborhood oneself. Even if we gossiped about each other a bit, that only made us more valuable in each others' lives; at least as sources of diversion and entertainment we would be loath to have taken away.

Winterset, probably like most small Iowa towns in the mid-twentieth century, had a self-contained aspect which gave it a sense of peaceful calm and security. We (at least most of the adults) knew about a lot of the less pleasant things going on in the wider world, but for the most part they didn't rile or contaminate the pleasant routine of small town life. One could count on Winterset being about the same in the morning as it had been the evening before, providing the comfort of a continuity which rarely threatened. The biggest change we experienced, with reassuring regularity, was the slow inexorable shift of the seasons.

And those seasons in Iowa, at that time, really did shift. Each had its own personality and one was absolutely never confused as to which season one was living in at the moment. Even the so-called 'shoulder seasons' gave us a rich taste of their distinctive flavors over a long enough period to savor them carefully. There was no merger of autumn and winter, or spring and summer, as too often seems the case nowadays. And each season stood its ground—winter was winter with no chance of being mistaken for a chilly early spring or an autumn hanging on a bit too long. Mid-summer was really hot and really humid, period, with no disconcerting ambiguity. The passage of time in Winterset could be trusted to stick with its assigned schedule and it rarely teased us with any hint of deviation—except, perhaps, for 'Indian summer' days; those brief autumn fallbacks into summer which constituted perhaps the most joyous season of all, and certainly the most colorful.

Am I painting too happy a picture of time in the Winterset of the mid-twentieth century? Too gentle a picture? Too easy, too forgiving? Too colorful? Well, you have to be the judge. But remember, I was there. ⌘

# 1 January
## A Love Affair with Snow

We had somehow claimed winter as our own; an orphan unwanted by the rest of the country busy naming its towns and cities for spring or summer.

Actually, we narrowly avoided the same fate.

When the town fathers met to name the place in the middle of the nineteenth century, in a little log cabin which now sits proudly in our town park as a memorial, the consensus favored "Summerset." One rugged old cuss, feeling the pull of his cantankerous breed and the sharp chill of the changing season, then made his contribution to the debate: "Damn well better call it 'Winterset.'" Bingo! We would not march with the legions of Springfields crowding the rest of the country. We would forge our stolid way bravely facing the cruelty of winter by embracing it.

Actually, if one were a school-boy around the era of the town's centennial celebration, winter was not cruel at all—it was a fantasy land of beauty and play, of sleds and snowball fights and snow forts and building snow men; of the pleasurable pain of red chaffed cheeks and noses; of writing on frosty windows with a finger; of watching fat icicles sparkle in the sun; and of returning to a warm home to hang wet socks on the radiator and drinking the hot chocolate Mom had brewed in anticipation of her little tribe's need for a recess.

Did we envy the rest of the world with its wide collection of Summersets and Springfields? They didn't cross our minds. We'd heard of faraway places that were supposed to be beguiling; of big cities with canyons made by skyscrapers and the icy winter winds which raced through them. We had our own canyons. Canyons with walls four, five, even six feet tall created when our dads shoveled the sidewalks clear of the snow that kept falling and never melted away until April or even May. We were kids reveling in our true heritage as children of the winter. I can't speak for the adults of the time, however.

At school, recess outside on the playground was the highlight of the day. Actually, that may not have been limited to winter, come to think about it. But winter did not diminish the allure of recess in any way. We'd bundle up,

## January

picking our coats from the heaps of scarves and mittens and boots which littered the school hallways, and race outside for another dose of that precious commodity: snow.

The little kids, the kindergarteners and first graders, would show off the ignorance of the world they still clung to by getting their tongues frozen to the metal bars of the jungle gym. The girls would make snow-angels. We somewhat older and more sophisticated third and fourth grade boys would play 'King of the Hill' from atop a mound of snow plowed from the school bus parking lot. Or we'd concoct races down the slope of the baseball field on the sleds we'd brought with us to school.

One winter recess in about third or fourth grade was the scene of perhaps my greatest grade school relationship triumph. When I'd moved to town at age four, my first new friend was a kid, Bobby, my age, who lived a couple of blocks away. We were fast friends all the way through our time in the Winterset school system. But for whatever boyish reason he had started at that stage the rather disconcerting habit of kicking me in the rear at any opportunity. Not kicking me hard enough to inflict real pain or do intentional damage, but doing it boldly and in full view of our peers; probably as some form of proving dominance or male bravado.

Anyway, at this particular winter recess, one recess too many for my putting up with Bobby's new hobby, I had a sudden masculine impulse of my own: self-defense and revenge. At the top arc of Bobby's kick I reached back with my left hand and grabbed his ankle, toppling him flat-backed into a snow bank. The shock on his face told me who the winner of the confrontation was, and that the kicking binge was finished. It told Bobby, I'm sure, something he had not expected about his shy friend who, even at that early stage, had set his sights on becoming a clergyman, the gentlest form of masculinity known to society. Bobby and I moved on then to more conventional forms of interaction.

For a school boy of that era, in the winter a sled was almost an appendage. We rode them everywhere, and when we couldn't ride them, we carried one along anyway awaiting the next opportunity. A sled was to winter what a bicycle was to summer. They came with us to school, and back home with us at the end of the day. On weekends they often filled our entire Saturdays.

We'd wake up to a wonder-land of epic proportions. Fresh snow covered everything outside and clung to every branch and every twig of every tree and shrub, glistening in the gold of the rising sun. No fairy land of imagination could have been more beautiful, more exotic, more inviting. But here it was, delivered free of charge by the gods of winter who dangled this splendor in front of little boys and girls knowing they had no power to resist; knowing they would be lured outside to frolic in the manna of winter's bounty.

After pulling on layers of clothing we'd rush outside to be reunited with our beloved sleds. We'd ride or take turns pulling each other past the town square where big tractors with front-loading scoops were shoveling snow into huge trucks to be hauled out of town, clearing enough of the streets to allow at least two narrow lanes of traffic.

Then we'd thread our way to the steepest hill at the edge of town to join friends in flying down to the bottom; even if we didn't know the other kids well, they were instantly allies in the all-important mission of the moment. Then we trudged back up the hill pulling the sled, maybe with a younger sibling hitching a ride, only to shove it off the precipice and belly-flop on again for another ride to the bottom—over and over, again and again, until we knew it would spell trouble if we didn't show up at home again soon, as the moon began to illuminate the snow, taking over for the retiring sun.

Another small handful of years and suddenly we were in the more demanding confines of Junior High School, which it seemed some other towns called Middle School. I stopped bringing my sled to school, which was now not just across the street, but entirely across town. It seemed easier and faster now to just walk through the snow, although I did note that a lot of the other guys were not yet weaned from their sleds and continued to arrive at school with them. Whether by then the sleds were serving as actual transportation or just totems of security I'm not entirely sure. I *am* sure that for half the year we were truly children of winter, and that it would take some decades to discover that winter could actually be uncomfortable and inconvenient.

## SUPERVISING OFFICER

Junior High presented new challenges and adjustments but there was one area of school life which went better than the others for me: Safety Patrol.

A few of the boys were appointed to be "Patrol Boys" and got to leave Junior High afternoon assembly early to take up positions at nearby street intersections. There they were to hold back the grade school little kids from crossing until there was an acceptable gap in traffic.

I was appointed the "Lieutenant" and my badge had an authoritative red background, compared to the mere silver of the regular Patrol Boy badges. There were no other ranks or officers so I was, in effect, really the Patrol Boy General. I didn't have to go out to the cold winter streets with the others if I didn't want to, but I could if I wished. I had the freedom to supervise proceedings at will.

## January

And being a freshly minted teenager who was as glad as anyone else to leave school a little early, supervise I did.

I never figured out how I added anything to the alertness or judgement of the regular Patrol Boys who did the actual work, but I was always out there "supervising" conscientiously. I suppose my greatest value to the system was actually that I was the designated substitute if another Patrol Boy missed a day of school because of illness.

Mostly my supervising consisted of going to my friend Craig's corner and chatting with him during gaps of student flow. Craig was my current best friend from the rotating ranks of best friends throughout our school days. Here was my big chance each day to leave my perpetual shyness behind, and to do it even with a bit of panache, with an almost John Wayne swagger, as the "supervising officer."

For some reason the only topic I remember from these on-duty chats with Craig was the day he pointed out that one little street-crosser always had a sore looking and icy upper lip because it was winter and he evidently constantly licked his lips. Maybe the reason I remember this exchange is because this kid eventually drowned in the spillway of our town water works where his father was the manager and where he lived in a town-supplied house. When I look back at winter in Winterset now from the perspective of many elapsed decades, I think of the little kid with the perpetual frozen upper lip and his sad demise—the only winter event from childhood which registers with heaviness rather than brightness.

Snow also had an economic benefit for guys my age because the town was home to a good many folks trying to enjoy a stress-less old age—folks who had been duly warned that snow shoveling could end up being the kiss of death. So clearing sidewalks or driveways was added to newspaper deliveries as the work of the season for boys my age. Some of us had a list of regular customers who would hold out until we could get to them, while others roamed the streets, shovels slung over their shoulders, hoping to find *ad hoc* work (to our financial benefit snow blowing machines had not been invented yet, or at least had not found their way to Winterset).

Although by now I can't swear to it, memory suggests a medium snow shoveling job could bring as much as a dollar, about the same wage as for mowing the grass on the same property during the summer. A few of the old timers probably felt we were gouging by demanding so much money, but they sighed, paid, and went inside to contemplate how expensive life was becoming and lamenting the passing of the Good Old Days.

# INTO THE ARMS OF TEACHERS

In a way, the Good Old Days had been gradually slipping away even from us grade school kids. We had found ourselves moving on to Junior High School and leaving the majestic old red brick North Ward grade school which had nurtured us from nap-taking toddlers to increasingly worldly sixth graders discovering a place which contained creatures called girlfriends and boyfriends. And we found ourselves leaving, too, one of the most exotic fire escapes I've ever seen attached to a building.

From the outside it was a large round silver tube which began at the wall of a large room on the second floor, descended along the side of the school building, and ended in an open mouth at ground level. Kids loved to enter it from street level and try to crawl up, but none were successful in reaching the top before losing friction and being spit out on the ground again. From inside the school it was a strange heavy square door a little above the floor, normally bolted and locked. On designated days of the school year, this odd tube was the star component of official fire drills.

Teachers would station themselves at the ground opening. Other teachers would supervise from the inside as we were ordered to line up and file into the big second floor room. Then, we were required one by one to fling ourselves into the mouth of the strange tube in a rhythmic procession, and consign ourselves body and soul to whatever fate the tube might have in store for us. Soon there was, indeed, 'light at the end of the tunnel' as well as two teachers ready to grab our arms as the tube spit us out into the air in a steady drumbeat of terrified, or giddy, little boys and girls. ⌘

# 2 February
## Unisex Valentines

Americans were egalitarian by constitutional requirement, and Iowans were nice (as I'll explain later) and definitely did not want to hurt anyone's feelings.

This evidently imposed a strange February ritual on classroom life wherein each student had to give a valentine card to every other student in the class. The avoidance of hurt feelings made some sense to me because I was a church mouse and had developed an appropriate Lutheran sense of guilt. But even though I was not yet at the stage of acquiring a girlfriend, I knew enough about 'romance' to find it a little odd that the boys were required to give Valentines to all the other boys, and the girls to every other girl.

Then there was the slight confusion of thinking that giving someone a Valentine was supposed to indicate that one at least *liked* the recipient. Love was not an issue yet, but certainly I did *like* some of my classmates in particular, of *both* genders. So why was I required to distribute Valentines to everyone, when I was only aware of liking some of them? Well, it was second grade after all, so evidently life was supposed to be getting more complicated.

It's true that we'd already been introduced, by official teachers' orders, to hand-holding. At least once a year we'd group together as a class for the long walk over to the high school building to see a movie travelogue. The teacher would line us up in pairs and instruct us to hold hands with each other to bind the group into a tight formation. But no one associated this physical contact with any voluntary hand-holding the future might have in store, so there were no romantic implications. And besides, we got to choose our walking partners so the person whose hand was in ours was usually a friend and of the same gender. Naturally we'd *want* to give a valentine to anyone we'd held hands with, even if that person were not of the opposite sex.

These big unisex Valentine classroom parties were at least good for business on the town Square. Our moms had to buy enormous bags-full of red paper hearts. Then we students would have to sit down at home and address one to each classmate from a list the teacher had provided to insure that everyone received the same number of expressions of—what? Love? At least the same number of assurances of the absence of overt hostility.

Then, after school, all these declarations of affection returned to our homes again where maybe they were put up in some kind of display by refrigerator magnets for a day. Soon they would mysteriously disappear and life could return to normal, i.e. liking some classmates more than others.

Making the trip home on Valentine Day as well was a big card over which we'd actually spent time decorating and writing things as an official school assignment. This extra large Valentine was for Mom. There never were such Valentines ordered to be made for our dads. Evidently dads didn't have feelings as sharply refined as moms, or as the classmates we really didn't especially like.

These Mom Valentines had started life a couple days in advance of the big exchange of paper hearts. We were instructed to ask our mothers what their favorite color was, and report back the next day at school. But don't give the secret away; don't let Mom know she would be getting her own big Valentine.

So I sneakily asked my mother what her favorite color was, totally confident that the answer would be, had to be, 'red.' The answer, however, was 'yellow.'

What! How is this possible? What kind of person does not like red above all other colors? Especially with Valentine's Day on the near horizon. I did dutifully comply with her bizarre choice, however, and presented her with a big hand-made yellow something which had to pass for a proper Valentine. After many years of assuming my own favorite color was red, I discovered that it actually was yellow and painted and wallpapered most of my adult homes in various yellows. Mom had not been a renegade after all; she'd been a pioneer in revealing her inner soul.

## PRAGMATIC ROMANCE

Was February, cold and frosty, actually the month of love? By the time we ascended a few more school class rungs, the teachers, at least, began to assume it was. School activities began to be organized on the premise that boys and girls wanted to spend their time with each other, and in specific pairs on top of that. Maybe they did. But if so, I was rather slow in getting the message.

## February

One of my Junior High adventures in fledgling romance occurred because a roller-rink evening had been planned for us. We were all to choose a date for this event. I chose someone (all I remember is that she was popular and pretty) and whomever the guy was with whom we were to double (again I can't recall his name) chose someone. So far the rules (school instructions, actually) were simple and easy to follow.

Then, in subsequent discussion, it came out that the girl I'd invited had a crush on the guy whose name I can't remember. No problem. In my remote and calculated distance from the emotions of the whole affair anyway, I simply suggested that we guys should switch girls for this party. Done. I had succeeded in treating romance as a dry thing in need of manipulation and pragmatic judgements and actions. This was enforced dating anyway, resulting from school orders rather than any stirrings of the heart. Since I was dating without any prompting from hormones, I guess it made sense to apply mental processes in lieu of the emotional ones which were still eluding me. But the whole process was as cold as February itself.

By early high school hormones were beginning to thaw the ice a bit, even though they had not turned me into a little Romeo. When my church youth group organized ice skating parties on a frozen farm pond, I was ready to cooperate. There was a girl from a near-by small town whom I therefore saw only on Sundays, but who was beginning to be too attractive for even me to ignore. So I experienced something I could assume was an actual date, gliding around and around on the ice holding on to a girl I was proud to be seen with and actually wanted to be with.

February was also my birthday month. Oddly, however, I have very few memories of related celebration. There was always a cake, as there had always been a cake for my brother's birthday the previous month. There were gifts of some nature as well because our mother was too generous not to want us to have the apparently universally prescribed birthday experience. The only birthday gifts I can remember clearly, however, arrived by post from Illinois. My dad's aunt had been designated my "sponsor" at my Baptism (the rest of the world would have called her my 'Godmother') and she dutifully marked every one of my birthdays by sending a gift. And because she was a Midwesterner intent on not hurting anyone's feelings, she also sent along a smaller gift for my younger brother at the same time.

Her gift giving persisted until high school graduation, at which time she sent me a sleek and stylish desk lamp in anticipation of my going off to college. Ironically, when my dad helped me move into my dorm room on the first day of college, he tried to carry too many things at once and accidently smashed the lamp into a door post. Luckily he was a master mechanic, and soon had the lamp looking as healthy as the day it arrived in Winterset.

As to birthday gifts from Mom and Dad, part of the rub was that both my brother's and my birthdays came so soon after Christmas. At Christmas my relatives all went for broke and did things to the limits of their capacities. By our birthdays some exhaustion had set in, as well as some need for economic recovery. This translated into a few very practical items masquerading as birthday presents. Perhaps you can appreciate why a schoolboy receiving new underwear as a birthday gift would repress the memory. But practical or not, something was always gift wrapped and accompanied the cake with its gradually increasing number of little candles.

I had only one official birthday "party" that I can remember. It was when I was probably turning about twelve or thirteen, a landmark which families back then seemed to mark something like a debutant coming out, even if most other birthdays didn't rate a similar degree of festivity. The recalled image is of my sitting at the head of the table for dinner with a group of kids roughly the same age. The trouble is that they didn't seem exactly to be the kids who really should have been there. Most, if not all, of them were acquaintances from church, so the dinner party seemed more like a Luther League meeting.

This was strange only because I had friends at school, mostly boys, and I don't specifically remember any of them at my birthday party. Had my mother hoped to surprise me and taken the easy route of inviting only the kids she knew of from church? Or had she consulted me and I was in one of the periods of being so shy that I could not deal with suggesting the kids I really wanted to celebrate with? Or, I suppose at my stage of life now, one has also to posit that I just can't remember the details with sufficient clarity any more. A little discouraging no matter how the guest list was assembled. That guest list, however, was populated by more girls than boys which may seem rather strange for a kid who would grow up to be gay. On the other hand, it may be exactly what some experts in the field would expect—the whole process can be full of apparent contradictions.

Sometime in the following months my best friend Doug demonstrated how an early teen birthday party really should be constructed—or at least his mother did. I was outside playing in our back yard when Doug's mother pulled up to the curb in front of the house. Out jumped Doug who ran over to me to hand deliver an invitation. I was invited to a "Douglas B13" party, the imagery cleverly taken from a newly developed military aircraft (manufacturer and plane ID number) and applied to his name and his approaching new age.

## February

The party itself was fun enough I guess, and consisted of activities which might very shortly down the road have been considered a little frayed—pin the tail on the donkey, etc. The odd thing about it was, however, that I'm pretty sure the guests were all boys. So my one birthday party had centered on girls, as I recall. Doug, however, who would grow up to be a husband and father of two sons himself, had only boys at his turning-teenage birthday party. Fortunately at that point neither of us wasted too much time trying to figure out the conundra life was tossing our way. ⌘

# 3 March
## My Life with Words

It was journalism class during senior year in High School which brought me into an odd and memorable encounter with our high school Principal. It also landed me in a strange detour around the newly emerging turf of the birds and the bees.

H. C. Miller was loved greatly (although always in a very formal and somewhat stiff way) by the many classes at Winterset High School which came through its doors on his long watch, before, during, and after my time there. I think he really cared for each and every one of us, but his manifest dignity forced us to look between the lines for any evidence of his affection.

The only rule was that we were never to use his actual given name. He was "Mr. Miller" or, in print, "H. C. Miller." But—everyone knew that the "H" stood for Henry. That, as it turned out, was the rub.

Although seniors, we were of course still just big kids—and that was probably the other rub. For us, April Fool's Day might just as well have been a national holiday, and there stood a long tradition at the *Husky,* our high school paper, of running an April first edition based on deception and loaded with all the corny jokes and verbal pranks that adolescents of the era could come up with. So, for the 1959 edition of the April Fool's *Husky,* we ran a spoof front page story with the headline "Henry Miller Resigns."

Oh, did I mention that every *Husky,* and I mean literally every single copy of each *Husky,* had to go to the Principal's office to be potentially censored before it could be distributed?

After cranking out the April first edition (in those days, in a relatively small high school, in a relatively tax averse community, we were limited to publishing on a mimeograph, so we did quite literally 'crank out' each page) it was clean-up time after we'd put our baby "to bed," as real journalists might phrase it.

I may have been alone in the high school journalism room—if others were there as well they have been permanently blotted out of my memory. There came a knock at the closed door. The editor went to the door to reply. Door opened. There in front of me, ram-rod straight as always, and with no hint of humor on his face, stood Mr. Miller holding a big stack of paper.

Plop—the entire current edition of the *Husky* was dropped on the floor in front of me and I could feel the burn of a major blush on my face. With a piercing stare, but without a word, Mr. Miller turned on his heel and was gone.

We were left to run an entire new edition of the *Husky* because we'd transgressed with just one word: "Henry."

On a subsequent visit to Winterset years later I went up the hospital hill to see the campus of the 'new' high school built long after the graduation of the class of 1959. There, engraved prominently on the outside wall of a building named to honor everyone's favorite high school principal, I read with disbelieving eyes: "Henry C. Miller Auditorium."

Journalism class in high school offered the great gift of helping to solidify a life-long love of words, and starting me on a path which led to college newspaper work, a brief editorial stint at a small national religion journal, and a several year career as a newspaperman at *The Star-Ledger* in Newark, then the seventh largest daily newspaper in the country. I truly loved the *Star-Ledger* job, even though I eventually went on to other things rather than making journalism my life's career.

Wise folks have speculated that we can't actually understand a concept unless we have a word for it. The word itself becomes the meaning and enables us to feel and visualize and explain the concept to ourselves; the word almost becomes tangible, and without that word (or name) the thing or the concept are just vague waifs struggling for bodies of their own. Words are what cements us into reality; words enable us to see and become an actual part of the world we live in.

I confess here and there in this look back at life in Winterset that I was a verifiable church mouse. Well, the Lutherans had their Word (capital 'W') in which they placed enormous stock, and by which they meant either the Bible, or Jesus himself, or St. John's "Logos," or preaching and sermons, or the creating dictum of the Almighty, anything at all written by St. Paul, or maybe several other highly conceptual and arcane theological ideas. Frankly I don't believe they actually ever really knew what they meant by "Word," or at least were never able to agree among themselves about what they meant. But they did cling to it and use it unsparingly.

Confusing, and sometimes disagreeable, as that was for me, I had my own words (lower case "w"). And these words were potent tools. They were powerful friends who showed me meaning and revealed truth. I've always needed to put something in writing before it became real to me.

After it became a word, or words, it lived; but before that it was a vaporous mere 'potential.' I didn't always know how to deploy these words to the greatest effect, and perhaps still don't, but I knew their potential could never be exhausted.

So, words were 'my thing,' but spelling them correctly in the English language never was (I've given Google lots of business trying to figure out spellings while writing the many words in this book—I read somewhere that being good at spelling was an indication of intelligence, a theory I've always felt was rather insulting because it called into question the level of my own intelligence). And I wasn't that great at verbal articulation either, unless the words were first put down on paper, as I was sure they should have been anyway.

I was sure that words were meant to be written and read, despite the fact that we could not carry on effectively without speaking and hearing them as well. (Later, as a clergyman, I had to write out in full detail every sermon. I might have been able to deliver some of it almost from memory later, but it absolutely had to be written out word-for-word on paper before there could be anything to deliver at all.)

## DOUBLE DATING AS A TRIO

Boys who hadn't figured out how to appreciate girls as much as the script called for could nonetheless be as resourceful as anyone else in working through romantic problems, and I had solved the problem of my weak attraction to girls while a high school senior by linking up with a boy—what else!

Larry (known universally as Butch) always sat at the desk just ahead of mine in journalism class, and we became best friends for that last school year. We also became partners in the newly serious business of dating girls!

Looking back I understand how this was the perfect solution for me, although I'm not at all sure what it did for Butch. We settled into a pattern of going to the movies in Des Moines as a double-minus-one date: He, me, and one girl. The rationale was usually that one or both of us guys could not get a date that weekend, and so we threw ourselves on the mercy of a kind girl who could then discharge her charitable obligation to mankind in a two-for-the-price-of-one setting.

The arrangement was just great for me. I was actually going on "dates," and for that matter going on dates which included a guy I liked. I still don't understand why Butch went along with this. Ironically, perhaps, as an adult he lived with his wife nearby to our usual "date" (Raejean) and her husband, another of our WHS classmates (Dick), and those four continued as great friends as the years went by.

## March

As senior year worked its way to conclusion there was indeed pressure to finally begin dating girls more seriously, even though the pressure was coming from my own self-image. I was still trapped in a hormonal gap, awakening increasingly to sexuality in a general sense but still less attracted to specific girls than I felt should have been the case. I was, as the song had it, "falling in love with love," which the lyrics went on to warn me was "falling for make believe."

Contradictory as it may sound, however, I'd had a sort of mini-crush on Diane since sixth grade when I noticed how this petite beauty dressed so wonderfully, and dressed so wonderfully femininely, compared to any other girls in the class. In the back of my mind therefore I had a theoretical girlfriend. I somehow managed, in my own vague way, to carry on a purely imaginary affair with her from sixth grade all the way through high school but never putting it to the test. I'd be surprised if Diane ever knew she had a role in my romantic life—heaven knows I gave her very few, if any, clues probably because romance felt a lot more comfortable to me as a theoretical state.

In the swirl of adolescence I wasted a lot of time taking other girls to proms and letting my eye rove. Since the girl in any "date" never really clicked with me anyway, why not move along and hope the next one would. So I never got around to asking Diane on a date. Looking back this all strikes me as complex in a Freudian sort of way, but in truth I think it was utterly simple: I really did have some kind of feelings for Diane, so she was much more threatening than girls whose attractiveness aroused less complex emotions.

Finally in senior year I figured out that she had not been dating any more seriously than had I (so far as I could observe), and that as much as I had always felt she was way above my league, maybe I should have paid more attention to her.

In senior year she and I were in journalism class together. I had been appointed editor of the school paper, the "Husky," as I've already mentioned, and was feeling a little of the pride that came with being a senior and having some standing in my class at long last. My journalism teacher did manage to bring me down to earth, however, when she told me "If I'd known you were not going to write an editorial in every issue I would have appointed someone else."

Nevertheless I was happier than in any earlier school grade, and part of our budding independence as late teens was the chance to spend some after-school hours working on the paper without teachers or parents present. One such day, stretching into evening, Diane and I were the only ones on duty.

I guess a more standard-issue type of guy than I would have flirted with the girl in a setting like that, or even have tried to kiss her. But I was not really a cookie cutter sort of guy. Then, suddenly in what must have been almost a divine intervention that particular evening, something excessively odd came over me which completely surprised me—I *wanted* to kiss her, myself, *me* (!), or at least I felt the instinct to go through the motions of wanting to, which felt so deliciously "adult."

What we ended up doing instead was racing through the dark hall ways, she ahead of me, me in hot pursuit but judiciously always a few steps behind, with her screaming at the top of her lungs. We were both enjoying it immensely, but God only knows why. It was more like a track meet than romance.

I'm sure neither of us had paused long enough mentally to figure out what we would do if I actually caught up to her. This game was fun for both of us precisely because it was so uncharacteristic for either of us—we were making up for lost time by acting like younger children, and at the same time exploring our sexualities in a fairly harmless and unthreatening way.

Suddenly the answer to the little enigma of what we would do if we caught up with each other appeared right in front of me in the form of Mr. Scott, the science teacher—we'd do absolutely nothing because I would not catch up to her, and I certainly should not have been chasing her through the hallways in any case.

Unknown to us, Mr. Scott had been conducting a night class and had gotten sick of the screaming. He came into the hall and dressed me down with the least kind thing he could have said, especially with Diane listening from a stairwell: "**YOU**, *of all people.*" Ouch. Not only had I misbehaved, but it seemed that Mr. Scott might not have considered me the type of guy who would *want* to chase a girl in the dark. Or maybe his reaction was based on my wanting to become a clergyman, which was known to the faculty by then. Either way my image in his eyes did not seem to be quite as red-blooded as I had been feeling a few moments earlier.

The testosterone, such as it may have been, evaporated and the evening ended with a whimper. Only much later in my dreams have I rewritten that ending, imagining just in fantasy that it ended with the kiss I think I really must have wanted that night.

Soon it was late in senior year, and our time was crowded in ways we were often experiencing for the first time. Diane and I had no real time alone together again until after a class graduation party hosted by Mike, one of our classmates, in the yard of his west end Winterset house.

## March

The party was non-alcoholic, no drugs, sprinkled with parents, and overall very tame by what seems to be the norm for adolescent parties today. There was probably plenty of food and sweet drinks. We talked as if we were already adults, and as if we had the world fully figured out already. Bob, my friend from even before Kindergarten, expounded on why sleep was a dreadful waste of time and how he planned to go through college not burdened with such sloth. We all felt the joyous thrill of starting to leave the limitations of childhood behind—Bobby was free to stay up all night and make himself sick doing it if he wanted to.

Diane and I left the party together, I'm pretty sure by some kind of telepathic mechanism. For some intangible reason we connected emotionally that evening, as I had always felt was somehow inevitable.

I offered to drive her home to her parents' house on their farm a few miles outside town. We walked slowly back to my house to pick up my dad's car, through the deserted town Square and the heady fragrance of the late spring air. The moment felt intimate and for some reason there was an opening for me to ask her if she had ever had sex (I think the actual words were much more delicate than that because the course of the conversation was mutual and gave us both all the context we needed to know exactly what territory we were exploring verbally).

She said "No" and I could almost feel her sweet blush, hidden by the growing darkness. I quietly said "me neither," and we kept walking, I at least, feeling somehow validated in that one of the cutest girls in my class had no more sexual experience than I did. And validated, too, because for the first time in my life I had engaged in an intimate moment with a girl; and not just any girl, but my long standing secret crush.

I guess it should have dawned on me that because this warm and lovely and exciting moment did not become also a physical moment, something was off-kilter between me and the opposite sex. But hiding from the gathering truth had become a much practiced specialty of mine by then, so I was skilled at pushing romance into the future where it could flower, as I was sure it eventually would, on its own time schedule.

I got Diane home in good shape and still a virgin, feeling somehow very adult, and not too troubled that I was going home still a virgin myself. College was just weeks away and life was so crowded and so full of potential adventure that it was unfortunately easy to forget to live in the moment—because we were so busy living in the future. But it was another situation which would have turned out differently for one of my male classmates (at least I supposed so), and another evening which has come back to me often in my dreams because of the path not taken. I should have been driving home having been at last, and at least, kissed by a girl.

And it should have begun to dawn on me that maybe I wasn't as eager to be kissed by a girl as I thought I was; or as I thought I should have been.

## TRYING TO BE JUST ONE OF THE BOYS

One of my ordeals in high school was supposed to have been a great honor bestowed upon me. Instead, it turned out to be another episode of wishing I could be just one of the boys but failing miserably in the attempt.

Each year the Winterset unit of the American Legion sponsored two high school juniors to attend Hawkeye Boys' State, a week-long affair held at the Iowa National Guard's primary camp, and at which the students would construct and elect a mock civic structure from coroner to governor, and polish their understanding of civic duty. (You can probably imagine to which office I was elected—no, actually it was a few steps above dog-catcher.)

Mr. Miller (H.C. Miller, please) nominated the candidates for the two Boys' State slots available. I don't know his criteria, but I was proud to be one of seven chosen that year. When the candidates met for instructions, Mr. Miller tossed out on the floor seven tiny folded scraps of paper. On five of these had been written inside "No" and on two "Yes." We were each asked to select one of these tiny paper things and unfold it.

Mine said "Yes." I knew immediately that spelled trouble, and I knew I did not want to attend Boys' State—much too masculine and oriented to athletics for my taste, or for my abilities.

I also knew that one of the "No" boys, Richard whom absolutely everyone called "Dick," actually really should have had the chance, and that he would be perfect for the role, and a proud representative for Winterset. He was our class president and later known as our class's "president of everything." Not only was he popular, but he was a genuine athlete who later spent his career as a school PE instructor and married the girl who 'double dated' with Butch and me.

Mr. Miller then gave the 'winners' a chance to reverse the verdict on themselves if they wished. I wish I'd had the courage and the generosity to yield my place to Dick, who really should have been one of the "Yes" boys.

But I was shy and hated making any sort of waves at all which would call attention to myself. And also, in truth, I was glad to have some recognition come my way at that point in school life. How could I turn it down, even when I suspected I'd hate the actual experience?

So I found myself arriving at Boys' State, picking a bed, and unpacking my stuff. When darkness and curfew arrived, do you think the barracks-full of teenaged high school boys were eager to get some sleep looking ahead to the eventful next day? I think eventually I *did* get a little sleep, but that was after all the shouts and whoops and verbal displays of hormones which I'm sure were not confined to this particular barracks, nor to my particular year at Boys' State.

And these were not just ordinary risqué jokes. This was sophisticated, top-of-the-line material! "So, I yelled to the girl caught on the other side of the gorge, 'I've got something here you could walk across on, baby.'" I should have been taking notes for all the future occasions when I might want to act the he-man myself. The two guys who seemed to be the leaders of this soiree were located one on each side of me—lucky me!

In the morning after coming back from the shower, I found my bed had been moved into the corner and my two loud comrades would henceforth be sleeping, peacefully, no doubt, directly side-by-side.

Then disaster struck. Each morning began with everybody called outside for a session of vigorous calisthenics as if we were already National Guardsmen. For whatever reasons, physical, emotional, psychological, lack of sleep, or just from sheer terror, I fainted dead away right on the exercise grounds. This, as you may suspect, was not especially helpful to my already challenged status in the barracks.

During subsequent such morning workouts I'd sneak away to find the other boy from Winterset, one of our several "Larry" classmates, and we'd sit on the grass and talk about whatever we talked about. It would appear he was not terribly fond of the workouts either.

Still I can't really say I didn't learn anything that week. One of the guys running for mock governor was giving his spiel about how "ideas are like babies, easy to conceive but difficult to deliver." So a touch of sex education got thrown into the mix—always theoretically a good thing. But who knew such rough and ready he-men boys talked that way!

Dick, the guy I thought should have gone to Boys State from Winterset instead of me, was a friendly presence for me during high school. But I think that was probably because he was a friendly presence for *everyone* in high school at the time. He and I were never especially close friends, yet I can rationalize saying we were friendly. And as life has plowed on I've discovered a link with him that binds us together strongly, even after his untimely death.

We are both totally rabid University of Iowa football fans (I'm referring to him in the present tense because a little thing like death hardly seems sufficient to blunt the bottomless depth of emotion felt by a true Hawkeye). Dick's wife once told me that during any game not proceeding according to plan, he could not even bear staying in the same room as the TV set. Dick had to preserve his sanity by stepping outside, even in frigid weather, to cool down.

I'm less sensible than that. When we're losing I hold on to the bitter end and then end up torturing the guys I live with by entering the foulest of moods. By Sunday afternoon I've usually regained some equilibrium and decided that life may still be worth living. But at first it's a very tenuous grasp on that idea.

Anyway, on a losing Saturday I suffer along with Dick. Many years after high school, and after Boys State, Dick and I somehow share a passion. That's when I miss him most. If only he could have at least seen that spectacular sixty yard kick-off return, and shared the fleeting vision that next week was bound to get better. And (fortunately for my sanity) next week usually did get better, and I've been blessed to live through a second golden age of Iowa football.

Meanwhile, Dick got the girl. The girl I was convinced I was dating during senior year, even though there were two of us guys vying for that honor at the same time and during the same 'dates'. And I know she was a worthy prize, to use some chauvinist language. So I do hope and expect that Dick had a happy life despite the catastrophic betrayal by the Iowa football team he had to endure on a number of Saturdays along the way.

Love can sometimes be a mixed blessing, contrary to our romantic notions. And it wasn't just life which taught me that. It was football too. ⌘

# 4 April
## Marshmallow 'Cheeps' & Jelly Beans

The grass was a vibrant green, but it consisted of shredded plastic. In this ersatz hay nested foil wrapped chocolate eggs, usually surrounded for good measure by jelly beans and yellow marshmallow chicks—a whole day's allotment of calories in one convenient basket, but fortunately I was not yet counting calories. Such an Easter basket awaited my brother and me each Easter morning for many school years, possibly owing as much to our parents having experienced the deprivations of the war so shortly ago as to their wanting us to enjoy the holiday.

April was the return of sunshine (interspersed with showers, of course), the renewed hope of spring, and the dyeing and hiding of Easter eggs. But it was also a heavy dose of religion—the last run of Lent with its mid-week extra services culminating in Easter Sunday which brought an unusual full capacity to the pews in our cozy brick church across from the high school. I was so tied to those Lenten Wednesday evening sessions of blood, suffering, guilt, and Godly self-sacrifice that I even tried my hand at using them for dating girls, which may give you something of a measure of my level of high school eccentricity.

Lutherans were one of the three largest Christian groups in Iowa during my day there. Methodists were the largest of the Protestant denominations, and we Lutherans came next in that category, mostly in the northern half of the state where the immigrant Scandinavian farmers who had nearly swallowed up Minnesota and the Dakotas spilled into our turf. Roman Catholics were the largest group, and had been so from our French roots as part of the Louisiana Purchase. The Archbishop of Dubuque, I'd learned while attending school there, had once held ecclesiastical authority for most of the western part of the country, right up to the California border. At least that was the story students passed to one another back then.

We were Lutherans of Germanic descent rather than Scandinavian, however, and were more concentrated in the southern part of Iowa. There was a concentration of such good people in Adair County to our left looking at a map, and the seeds of Lutheranism in Winterset were sowed from that colony.

My family had moved to Winterset from Ames, where my brother was born and where my father worked for the government lab at Iowa State University (then "College") which was at that time helping develop the atomic bomb during the war (the "Manhattan Project").

I could never learn much about Dad's work there because he was sworn to secrecy, but whatever it was (I'm sure it involved welding, because it was his prowess in that field which the government needed enough to give him government work instead of drafting him to fight in WWII), it gave our father a dark aura of intrigue and flare to his delighted young sons—he wasn't just a small town machinist, he was secretly in on big government affairs and a hint of cloak-and-dagger wafted around him. Looking back now I imagine his own feeling was one of pain to have needed to be part of something so ultimately horrible; but that generation did its duty despite the pain. The only hints I have of his work now are contained in a framed letter of commendation from the Secretary of War (now Defense).

It was in Ames that my mother took on her husband's religion, setting the course for a strict family observance. It was there also, as a result, that I was propelled on a career in Lutheranism which culminated with me as the pastor of a church in New York City. A career which closed there as well, when I gradually outgrew the boundaries imposed by non-stop Lutheranism and religiosity.

I remember being taken by my mother, as a three-plus-year-old, to a dinner for her confirmation class in Ames. I was in a chair between my mother and a young man who must have been a member of the confirmation class as well.

We were called to prayer pre-meal. The young man did not exhibit a physical stance of which I could approve under those circumstances. I turned to my mother and said (hopefully not too loudly), "He should be doing this," as I folded my hands primly in the artistically sanctioned mode. I was not only starting my career as a churchman, but if that pious little display was any indication, I was dangerously close to starting a career as a jerk as well.

When my family arrived in Winterset a little group of Lutherans transplanted from Adair County, including friends and relatives of my parents, had only recently organized a congregation. They met for services in a two story white frame house across the street from the (now former) high school, and housed their newly called pastor and his wife on the building's second floor.

## April

I was one of the very few young children in this congregation, and thus had to do double and triple duty for all the things children were supposed to contribute to church life at the time, like acting out the Christmas manger story and singing solos in timid and frightened little squeaky voices. "Vacation Bible School," that required staple of religious education, was held upstairs in the pastor's residence where I can't honestly remember any other classmates, although there must have been a few at least. I do remember winning a VBS prize for doing or memorizing something—a big jumbo version of a Baby Ruth candy bar, the largest single piece of candy I'd yet seen, and perhaps have seen to this date.

Eventually the congregation grew a bit and plans came into place to move the white house up the hill on the double lot where it would become in total the pastor's residence. A new handsome but not terribly large brick church would be built on the old site, a building which would become the focus of my remaining years in Winterset, at least if one doesn't count home or school. The construction of this building was accomplished by volunteer young men recruited from around the country by the national denomination as an experiment in helping struggling little Lutheran outposts.

Naturally, my mother enthusiastically volunteered to host two of these guys and so for months on end our family consisted of six members, and I had, in effect, two older brothers. Unfortunately I was young enough not to fully appreciate any potential advantages this may have offered, or maybe I was just too young for these guys to have wanted to pay any attention to. In any case they finally left and I missed out on the experience of having older brothers, even if it had been only temporarily.

There were not many church related aspects that eluded me, however, during my early years, including meetings and activities of the Women's Missionary Society (or was it Ladies' Missionary Society?). Anyway when I was young enough that Mom couldn't leave me on my own, I was taken along as a kind of honorary member and got to hear some of the upstanding conversation exchanged, and observe the drinking of lots of tea and coffee. I'm not entirely sure what the official purpose of the organization was—probably something noble like encouraging native women in New Guinea to put on bras before attending Bible study sessions. Whatever the overarching purpose was, it did involve a lot of coffee drinking and gossip.

These meetings moved around to the various homes of the women/ladies involved, which often gave me country gardens to explore while the women/ladies deliberated. It also gave me tidbits of gossip and community news to try to put into perspective, such as the thinly veiled and excited discussion at one rural meeting of an evidently especially messy suicide the county had just experienced. I didn't draw too many conclusions from these meetings except that obviously the work of the Lord was being done, and that obviously doing the work of the Lord involved lots of chatter and coffee.

But, in fairness, whatever the work of the Lord was, these women were always about it and sometimes in ways that even I could dimly comprehend. The ladies were fond of staging what they called "Rummage Sales," for example.

These resembled what in later life I would think of as "tag sales," or perhaps on a grander scale, "flea markets." They would take place behind the huge display windows at the Ford dealership a block off the Square, where outgrown clothes and discarded household items would be offered for bargain prices to aid the building of our new church structure. As I recall, this essentially involved piles on the floor of women's purses, shoes, and so forth which customers then would 'rummage' through until they discovered a treasure for which it was worth parting with a dime or a quarter.

After the new church was built, the ladies of the missionary society became involved in an even more grandiose scheme which had huge piles of stuff heaped in all corners of the basement. This time the stuff was not for rummaging through, but for packing into large shipping boxes headed for our denomination's missionary fields in New Guinea. The ladies collected all manner of non-perishable domestic supplies, stockpiled them, and then spent happy hours packing them into crates to begin their journeys to the dark fields of the south Pacific island our particular denomination seemed so concerned about. I don't recall seeing any bras being packed, so I can't say exactly what the emergency was.

Anyway, through thick or thin, my mother was always on the front lines of these churchly eleemosynary activities, and always ready to report for duty no matter what the call. Save once. It was the middle of the first week of daily Vacation Bible School, and of course my mother had volunteered as a teacher. I was in my customary role as devoted student of stories from the Old Testament which seemed not to teach very much except that God was capricious and was busy both giving and taking with great alacrity, with maybe a little smiting tossed in for occasional extra color.

A rain storm of Biblical proportions soaked the town overnight and left our basement flooded up to several feet in depth. Dad rigged up a pump to pull the water out and dump it back into the already flooded ditch alongside the railroad tracks from which the water had probably seeped in the first place. There was work to be done; a washing machine to be saved; rows

## April

and rows of canned fruits and vegetables to be rescued. But—we were expected at the church.

So Mom, with me trailing along, walked in the continuing rain over to the church (why the family car was not utilized I'm not sure, except that maybe it too was flooded, and we did not yet have a telephone) to tell the pastor we would have to bail out of VBS that day because we had to bail out our basement. As I recall he was not impressed with the excuse, and sniffed the air as if offended at our abandonment of the Lord's work.

The next day when we returned to duty, however, the flannel graphs were still in place waiting to illustrate how Noah managed to stuff a zoo's worth of animals into a big boat to save them from another of God's watery caprices. So evidently we had inflicted no permanent ecclesiastical damage from our own great flood experience.

The irony of being taught all those Biblical stories as a kid is that as an adult I've studied the folklore and cultures (largely Egyptian) out of which they grew and concluded they have no more relevance to life today than the fairy tales we were also taught at that age—actually, maybe less, since the fairy tales do hint at some universal wisdom. Exactly the opposite outcome than was intended by the pious German Lutherans who struggled with Noah and his flood plus a host of other Old Testament characters. And that was the additional irony, daily Vacation Bible School was strictly a matter of 'Old Testament' content. A neutral observer could never have guessed that the folks running VBS considered themselves to be Christians. It might have seemed a more logical guess that the little brick church was actually the synagogue Winterset never actually had. ⌘

# 5 May
## Baskets of Violets

May had its folkloric baskets too, just like April, and they were called in true no-nonsense Midwestern argot "May Baskets." I discovered and started to assemble and give May Baskets because I'm an amateur botanist at heart. I'd like to tell you it was because I was starting to get sweet on girls in my class and wanted to give them a touch of spring for that reason. I did start to give some of them May Baskets, but it was because of the violets which were by then blooming profusely; because of my love of blooming plants rather than because of my love of the recipient girls themselves, alas. Nevertheless I loved searching for little early May flowers to arrange with a few jelly beans and present to the objects of my manufactured adoration.

Perhaps contrary to the impression I just gave you, I had acquired a technical "girlfriend" by then, Betty (technically only because she was a girl, I was a boy, we became friends, I thought I needed a girlfriend, and she thought I wanted to be her boyfriend). Our "dates" consisted almost entirely of playing on the school-yard swing set, riding the swings back and forth next to each other while talking about the things sixth graders talked about—or at the time perhaps just what I *thought* sixth graders talked about.

What Betty and I talked about was often my confirmation class, then currently in the process of turning me into a confirmed Lutheran who knew a lot of stuff, both sort of interesting and sort of silly or utterly pointless, not known to most of my peers.

In said confirmation class we were required to memorize Luther's small catechism, and then to recite it from memory in front of the congregation on Confirmation Sunday, before totally forgetting it in a few weeks, to our probable relief. In the moment, however, I was proud of accomplishing this dubious feat. So I would show off for Betty by reciting Luther from memory.

She, in turn, would exclaim what a marvelous thing it was that I could do this. And she would stare at me with those doughy and needy eyes by which many a boy has found himself being stared at by a girl, and absorbing the adoration as a masculine right.

## May

Somehow the school adults had noticed our apparent romance and we were now, in their official eyes, girlfriend and boyfriend. We were the advance party for the social structure which would manifest itself more universally a few weeks later in Junior High.

So, when a history of our class was written (by a teacher) and needed to be read out at a Junior High School assembly, the honors went to Phil and Betty.

We sat at a little table on stage and read into a primitive microphone which had to be hand-held. I held the mic for Betty, and soon a terrible shriek pierced through the hitherto quiet of the room. I had let the mic tilt in my hand, unaware that the thing had a mind of its own when it came to equilibrium. The art teacher had to join us on stage to solve the problem by un-tilting my hold on the mic.

But while officially having a girlfriend before most of my male classmates did was briefly ego-boosting, Junior High School was rapidly becoming for me a period of intense agony. The shyness which had always been part of my personality started now to spiral downward into despair and incapacity.

We used to be treated to 'field trips' in Junior High, usually to some place in Des Moines—the waterworks park, a Christmas model railroad display at a big church, the statehouse, a commercial dairy where students swiped their fingers with butter to lick behind the teacher's back—and one day we were headed on an outing to Des Moines to visit the local amusement park with its plethora of rides and other distractions.

The arcade contained machines which would issue black and white photos for a coin—the intrigue was that they were a mystery until they came out of the slot; you never knew in advance what the photo would contain. It baffles me now why this interested me, or why I saw these mystery photos as a good investment for whatever little money I had to dispose of, but by the time we were headed to the buses for the return trip to Winterset I had amassed a nice handful of them.

Rodney was my seatmate that day. He would be a difficult guy to sum up in a couple of words; not especially an athlete, not especially a brain, just a nice regular guy whom I always liked even though we never had an extended "best friend" period in school, or if we did it was mostly confined to walking up to the Square together over several years after each school day closed. His grandparents had a jeweler's shop just off the Square along an obvious route to my home, and Rodney always headed there rather than to his home; perhaps because his parents worked in Des Moines. It was not a long walk, but it did afford enough time to glue us together as good, if not intense, friends.

On the bus Rodney set about looking though my stack of photo cards, and landed on one of a Tarzan-like figure with a loin-cloth covering what we would later have termed in those days a "big package."

"How many children do you think *he* has?" Rodney asked with admiration in his voice.

A lot can shoot through one's brain in a split second. First I considered saying something to the effect that I doubted size had much to do with the answer to his question. But that would have been a kill-joy reply and would have made me sound more like a schoolmarm than a buddy.

In the end I was incapable of the sort of retort I imagined would be typical of any of the other guys in our class. So I bunted, and merely said "What?" as if I hadn't heard his question. Rodney, with a mix of exasperation and disbelief replied, "Oh, forget it."

I'd once again been willing to sacrifice a precious "just one of the guys" moment because I was too shy to jump into this mildly titillating circumstance. There was nothing unusual about two teenaged boys chatting about a topic like this. The "facts of life" had already been sufficiently hinted at in school health class (at least in broad terms—the it takes both a male and a female together part), and whatever remained of those mysteries had pretty much been filled in by guesswork and hormones. There was no guilt involved in talking with a peer about things all of us were thinking about in any case. In fact, we were supposed to be bonding with each other by virtue of sharing our discoveries and theories. So not eagerly plunging into sex talk was not really how Junior High School was supposed to go, but it was indeed how it went for me.

This shyness thing was beginning to be a serious problem. It was almost as tangible as the occasional new hair beginning to make cameo appearances on various body parts, and it felt like an illness of some sort; which indeed it may have been.

Social Studies was a course in Junior High School which I really liked, and I really liked the teacher. Yet my hand was always glued to my side when questions were proposed to the floor, and it's possible I emerged from the whole seventh and eighth grade years without ever having said one word out loud in that class—or maybe in any class at all for that matter.

Mid-way through the year at a parents-teachers event, this Social Studies teacher pulled my mother aside and explained how much more effective these student days would be for me (including for my grades) if I'd speak up and participate in class.

She relayed this concern carefully, faithfully, and gently. I got the message and it rang true; I already knew it was true and had told it to myself many times before this. But a few days later when the teacher stopped me and asked if my mother had explained things to me, I looked down at the floor and softly said one word: "No." I was capable of betraying even my own mother because I was not capable of defeating the iron grip by which shyness then controlled me.

Just after entering Junior High School, or Middle School, I left church with my family one Sunday morning and we headed as usual to Benoit's, the mid-sized neighborhood grocery where many Winterset folks shopped for Sunday lunch after services. In those days, Sundays meant dressing up in one's "Sunday best" for church; no sneakers, no open necked shirts, and most certainly no shorts.

So there I was getting out of our car wearing a blue blazer, with a pink dress shirt, and a (clip-on) black and pink bow necktie. I thought I looked rather rakish. We ran into the Junior High Principal on his way out of the grocery store, and he kindly stopped to compliment me: "Wow, you look like you just stepped out of an issue of *Gentleman's Quarterly*." My mother, being proud, as mothers are of their offspring, replied, "Yes, and he earned the money for his clothes all by himself."

I averted my eyes. Later, in the car: "Mom, please don't say things like that. It makes us sound poor." At that age, I think, any parental response would have been grounds for embarrassment, and any topic whatsoever held great potential for embarrassment.

In eighth grade the teachers came up with an entertainment plan for the next parents-teachers event. They would stage a competition between a panel of parents and a panel of students in which questions would be posed by a teacher-moderator. The panelists were supposed to buzz as quickly as possible if they knew the answer. The plan was for the kids to give the parents a real run for their money.

To determine which students would sit on the quiz panel, the entire student body was administered a test designed to find out who could score highest in general knowledge—a bit of history, a bit of sports, a bit of math, etc.

A day later the announcement of the overall winner of the general knowledge test came at our regular assembly. The Principal stood in front of us saying that (what! No, please!) Phillip Truckenbrod had turned in the highest score. A little twinge of pride shot through me, followed by a much longer agony—now I would have to take the stage at the parents-teachers quiz show.

The evening inevitably arrived, and I sat there on the panel not buzzing.

Answer after answer which I knew perfectly well flew past without my speaking a word or lifting a finger. When the moderator asked one direct question to each panelist, the answer to my question was "Calvin

Coolidge". I said "Alvin Coolidge." The kid with the most general knowledge in Junior High now stood before the world looking like the dimmest kid in Junior High.

You knew the answers to this, and to that, didn't you, my mother asked me when we got home. Yes, I did. But my shyness, as always it seemed, was in absolute unwavering control. To buzz would have called attention to myself—if one is crippled by shyness, that's the last thing in the world one wants to do.

Eventually the shyness faded and I've been able to lead a reasonably normal life. Several adult years were even spent as a clergyman, which placed me essentially 'on stage' constantly. Yet something like that never disappears completely, and keeps lurking in the background as a kind of souvenir of the torturous days of Junior High School. ⌘

# 6 June
## The Birds & The Bees

Clark Tower is a monument to a pioneer era family in Winterset's city Park, three levels high counting the top roof with its crenulated circular half wall. It was built of field stone, and one reached the second floor via an attached outside stone stairway which wrapped half-way around the tower, and the top level via a metal ladder inside the second level. It was open to the weather and the world; public property with no doors. Just the kind of castle-like fortress designed to capture the imagination of school boys, and probably school girls as well.

Winterset in those days was an open playground where kids were allowed to wander wherever the wind blew. No one could imagine why there should be any fear for our safety, and parents probably thought all that freedom was good for building our characters. So the city park became a much frequented area for my little circle of friends, with no area of it more intriguing than Clark Tower, grandly proclaiming the highest point around town and surveying the river valley below in near-Medieval splendor.

Who came up with the rather eccentric idea of a sleep over in the tower I'm not sure at this point. Nor am I sure just who was involved, only a few boys, or were the usual girls actually allowed to join us. At any rate, our parents seemed to have no objections.

We set up camp in the middle level of the tower, with just blankets on the concrete floor for sleeping. To get into the middle level, however, we had to step over what appeared to be a pile of droppings from a large dog (except none of us thought it could have been a dog). Later from the top we saw a large Bobcat emerge from the woods into the clearing around the tower and then, when he sensed us, re-enter the woods. We took that as the explanation for the pile at the entrance to the middle floor, yet did not have the good sense to go home.

In any case the sleep-over in the tower was a one-time event, but the tower itself remained a beacon drawing our attention to the back roads of the park. We loved to hike all the way up to the site of the tower, possibly more than a mile into the park on a narrow gravel road, almost just a path, and I'm sure these occasions, at least, did involve mixed groups.

On one particular warm early summer day, the two girls in this particular hiking group decided they wanted to go topless on the return trip down the long trail from Clark Tower. So they dropped back a few feet from the two boys (me and someone I can't remember specifically at this point) and demanded of us, "Don't turn around; don't look back."

On its face the sentence was simple, clear, not in the least ambiguous, and apparently issued as an order: "Don't look back." Yet it was the most inscrutable sentence I'd yet heard in my dozen or so years.

*Clark Tower in city park, a boyhood mecca (photo: Teddi Yaeger)*

Was it really an order? Was it a plea, because boys couldn't be expected not to look anyway? A challenge? A warning? A threat? Maybe it was a taunt or a tease. Maybe it was even an invitation or a coded instruction; a plea turned upside down and running in the opposite direction—a "please don't throw me into the briar patch" kind of reverse psychology designed to capture the attention of male eyes. Maybe the girls wanted to titillate the boys because they were titillated at the idea themselves.

The first thought to hit me was that apparently I was *supposed* to at least *want* to turn around and look. That idea might not have occurred to me on its own, without the "suggestion" by the girls.

But soon there was a little rush of something else, something like pride—I had been regarded and treated by females like a man, or at least like a male. It had been assumed that my natural instincts would almost require that I look back, so that must mean that I was a real red-blooded boy; a handsome stud in the making—the sort of guy a girl would someday *want* to see her topless (assuming that was not already the case as we walked in the gentle embrace of early summer).

But I didn't look back. I don't believe my companion did either.

Did that mean I had fantastic self-control; that I was tremendously courteous and considerate, and that I respected girls as my mother had told me was required of me. Or did that mean I'd failed some sort of masculinity test? Did that mean I'd upheld the girls' faith that boys could be trusted, or did it mean I'd disappointed their assumption that I'd give them the little sexual thrill of taking a peek. Or, more strangely, did it mean that I didn't care enough to turn around, or weirder still, that maybe I didn't *want* to look back.

I could not decipher what the girls wanted to tell me. Probably it was as simple as it sounded when the words first reached my ears, but suddenly there were other factors weighing in; factors which were suddenly springing up from inside; factors which had never asserted themselves this way before. Maybe I was just happy with my little world as it was and not ready yet to walk into the complications that loomed ahead.

So we hiked on, descending down the twisting gravel road to the playground and picnic area of the park. The late spring sun was warming our faces (and some other areas of the girls' anatomy, I assumed), we were enjoying the freedom, the adventure, of just being alive. The birds kept singing. The bees kept buzzing. The world didn't seem to have skipped a beat. But there was now a little cloud in my mind I hadn't bargained with before. Evidently I was not going to escape, after all, the complications of that still mysterious force they called 'sex.'

I guess this fledgling 'sex in the park' episode may have altered my sense of the possibilities of the place, although the whole subject remained equally as intimidating as it was beginning to be intriguing.

A later such hike up to Clark Tower also involved nudity but required much less decoding, in that we were just a group of five boys, including my brother. From the tower there was a good view of a flowing river in the valley below. It beckoned enticingly on this hot day, with probably the stirrings of hormones making their as yet still subtle contribution. "Let's go play in the river," I suggested to a ready group of companions, undoubtedly feeling the same impulses and the same enticement of the sun.

We climbed down the steep hills, this time without the neat gravel path we'd used to climb up to the tower. We reached the river's embankments with their small reaches of beach-like shoulders covered with small stones and shaded by overhanging trees. Luckily we had *not* brought bathing trunks because no circumstance for needing them had been foreseen.

At the river we carefully folded our clothes, including our underwear, so that no tell-tale mud or other signs would present themselves later to our detective mothers, and we carefully laid them on rocks by the river bank. Into the water we waded, and we freely splashed around happily in our birthday suits—and I, for once, found myself doing what generations of country boys had enjoyed routinely and with carefree abandon, and only feeling *mildly* guilty about it (what if our mother divined the truth even without mud on our underwear?). Was this as close to Eden as one could get? It was boy-Eden, then, at least.

This time there was no cloud, no inscrutable instructions, no nudity which needed to be hidden or explained. There were just boys being boys in the most wholesome and innocent way—the most Iowa way—that linked us to country boys of untold generations past and future.

School was out for the summer and we were taking full advantage. But we were also rushing headlong into an increasingly adult world where one acquired responsibilities which didn't turn off for the summer like tripping a switch. So back in town I headed for the newspaper distribution room in the back of the florist shop near the Square. The papers had been trucked in from Des Moines on schedule and were waiting for the delivery boys to pick up their allotments. This was the partner paper of the *Des Moines Register*, the evening *Des Moines Tribune* (long ago discontinued). The daily papers were much smaller than the Sunday edition with its various specialty sections, so delivery was less like weight training and a little faster.

While I can't speak for my colleagues in this school-boy business, I never resembled the prevailing delivery-boy stereotype riding his bicycle down the street tossing rolled up papers in the general direction of houses and landing several on the porch roof instead. I left my bike at home after collecting my supply of papers and walked into my route territory on foot. Nor did I toss the papers casually toward the front door. I always, summer or winter, climbed onto the porch and placed the newspaper behind the screen door so that it was easily available to the household dry, and reachable without the need for being fully dressed. No one had coached or required this level of service, in fact no one had instructed us in anything other than to be sure to come in on Saturdays ready to pay for the papers we had distributed during the past week.

This rather fastidious method of newspaper delivery had actually been something I'd practiced for some time in advance. My very first income producing jobs had been delivering advertising circulars for the Ben Franklin five-and-dime store. Evidently store owners could save money by hiring local boys to hand deliver such printed material rather than sending it through the postal system. I have no idea what the postage tab would have been, but I do remember we were paid the handsome sum of one full penny for each circular we delivered.

At first several boys were hired to cover the whole town, and each of us had a specific neighborhood to cover. There were always stories of bundles of these advertising circulars being found somewhere in a gutter. This always made me even more scrupulous in my work, and not only did each and every one of the papers entrusted to me end up at a particular house, but tucked behind a screen door for easy retrieval and safety from wind or rain. And the reward was not only a clear conscience, but my first business promotion—as I grew a bit older, the Ben Franklin store hired me to cover the entire town. No longer would piles of the advertising circulars be found dumped *en masse*.

My particular newspaper route began just diagonally across the corner from our house, although I'd inherited it not because of geography but because it was the only one open when I became old enough to apply. Off the top of my head I'd guess now that my customer base probably hovered between twenty and thirty households.

This side of town was, to be honest but unnecessarily blunt, the poor end of town, which significantly limited the number of households which could indulge in the luxury of a daily newspaper. It could also be a bit aesthetically discouraging because of the ramshackle nature of many of these houses and front yards, with some of those front yards displaying the skeletal remains of seemingly every vehicle the residents had owned for years running. At the far end of the route sat a small house trailer, home to a youngish couple who managed to pay their bill almost every week.

One Friday or Saturday the man, instead of merely giving me the $1.50 or so due for the week, seemed to want to engage in a bit of conversation. It turned out he and his wife were the managers of one of the two supermarkets in our town's central business area, the chain Thriftway store just a half block off the Square. Would I like to work for them at the grocery store? They had an opening for a 'stock boy.' I talked this over with my parents and the answer turned out to be an enthusiastic, "Yes, I would."

An older boy who worked at the store showed me the ropes on my first afternoon on the new job. We were stocking cans of soup into the shelves on the far aisle when suddenly bits of ice started to pelt the floor around us in a sort of rhythmic pattern. I must have started, but my new friend said, "Oh, never mind. That's just Shocky over in the meat department." Shocky evidently was exercising his throwing arm not for the first time. A couple days later I bought a bag of cookies from the store and offered some to all of my new colleagues. When I got back to Shocky behind his gleaming white, glass fronted refrigerators, he gushed with gratitude and extolled my generosity loudly to the whole store as though not the remotest hint of kindness had ever crossed his path before.

Working at the grocery store offered a behind the scenes education to the food handling business. In the back room where deliveries came in, I was assigned on only the first or second day of work, to help the manager's wife open crates of cabbage heads. This involved, to my surprise and discomfort, peeling off the top layers of the cabbages by hand and discarding them, along with the squiggling worms they were feeding, into big garbage cans. Then placing the remaining heads in the fresh produce section for unsuspecting mothers shopping for dinner.

So my newspaper route opened the door to increasingly responsible jobs. Unfortunately, however, I had quit the newspaper delivery business so that I could put in the after school hours my new job at the grocery store required. After a few weeks it was announced that the company was going to close the Winterset store for lack-luster business levels, and I for the first time learned the frustration of being out of a job only a few weeks after learning for the first time the security of having a regular paying job.

I suspect my boss knew the store would close when he hired me. At least he knew it was hovering in jeopardy, so I experienced a flash of resentment that I'd been lured away from a little business which was made to order for a kid of my age, and then left high and dry. The managers moved on to another assignment at a different store of the chain in another town so they were okay.

I was left a little stung, but gradually accumulating some worldly wisdom. I had also started to save money while on that first job, and had accumulated the astronomically high sum of $30 by the time the axe fell.

Prudence must have been trying to set in, because I decided to open an account at a savings and loan establishment in Des Moines and start earning some interest on my nest egg. The plan, very rationally, was to leave all that money in the account and not touch it until the unfathomably distant future when I surmised I might want to retire myself, as people eventually seemed to do with some regularity. When the later teen years arrived I had lost a lot of my prudence, as well as a lot of common sense, as teenagers tend to do. There suddenly were too many needs for money to resist touching my little nest egg any longer. It would be fun to know how much money I would have ended up with from that small seed had the plan been followed to its intended conclusion as, at this point in retirement, I sincerely wish it had been.

## June

The Thriftway job did, however, open doors to eventual continued employment in the grocery business when I landed a job at the supermarket around the corner on the Square itself. This store was owned by the father of one of my classmates, Craig, with whom I shared one of the 'best friend' periods during Junior High School. Here too was a back room where the job landed me a good deal of the time, and this back room held its revelations as well.

After school, at the start of one of my early work days at this new store, I entered the back room as one of the older boys was opening a carton of white cottony looking things. He held one up, taunting me and one of the other younger guys. "Do you know what this is?" he laughed. "I call them 'Peter Cheaters'." I sort of did know what it was, and yet I wasn't exactly sure at the same time. The only thing I was sure of was that those pesky Birds and Bees had caught up with me again. And it looked as though they had no plans to retreat from the scene. ⌘

*The author during his Winterset era: just before moving to town (above), his high school graduation portrait 1959 (top left), and as an early university student (left)*

# 7 July
## Parades, Fireworks & Picnics

July was suffused with light.

The generous daylight allotment allowed kids to go outside after dinner for what seemed almost another day of play. And when darkness finally did settle in, we spent more time chasing lights that flitted about turning themselves on and off. Of course we tried to capture those 'lightening bugs' (or 'fire flies') and place them in jars whose lids we had punctured with air holes. Before bedtime we most likely turned the creatures free again, probably at the urging of mothers who explained that insects made very poor pets.

The most memorable lights of July, however, came from fireworks.

Fourth of July in Winterset was small town American life at its most wholesome and engaging, and probably also its most stereotypical.

My Dad would splurge by going to the "ice house" (yes, there was still a business which just made and sold ice) where the proprietors kept a big chest filled with water, ice, and pop (and yes, it was always "pop," never soda or even soda-pop). Dad would bring home a great selection of bottles: root beer, strawberry, orange, etc., almost as much fun to look at as to actually drink. But drink we did, of this sugar bomb liquid (artificial sweeteners had yet to be invented, or at least to be widely deployed).

I can't imagine how I escaped diabetes from this childhood of pop, nickel candy bars from Mrs. Mack's mini-grocery across the street, of homemade ice cream in the summers and always on the Fourth of July, of the enticing deserts which were an obligatory finish to every Midwestern meal of any significance whatsoever, and of the ubiquitous salads of the church pot luck dinners and family gatherings.

In case you don't speak Iowa, I'll translate—a "salad" was seldom a matter of greens (and when it was green it was either a wedge of iceberg lettuce or green "Jello"), but was almost always a molded gelatinous concoction which usually contained mini-marshmallows, but upon rare occasions might also include diced vegetables—think of an aspic where the primary ingredient is sugar.

## July

But back to the Fourth of July, when the corn was already knee high and only the most sophisticated folks would jeopardize their common folk credentials ('street cred') by calling it "Independence Day."

The mid-day meal invariably revolved around home-grilled hot dogs and/or hamburgers, washed down with ample 'pop,' and chased by homemade ice cream of many imaginative fresh fruit flavors. As I grew, it became my job to crank the ice cream machine, to rotate the core cylinder which contained the cream, sugar, and fruit, around and around in the mixture of ice, salt, and water which surrounded it. This job became more and more difficult as the ice cream began to form, because there were rotor blades meeting increasing resistance inside the cylinder in order to mix the thickening contents. It became hard work and sometimes an adult would need to finish up the job for me.

Winterset in my day always filled the town square with a travelling carnival on the Fourth of July—rides including a Ferris wheel so hastily put back together after the previous stop that the thrill came more from defying death than the view from the top of the wheel. There was always a Merry-go-Round (I remember the year I began to feel too old for this kiddie thrill, and the pathos of taking what I knew would be my very last ride); cotton-candy machines; booths where one could spend a lot of quarters failing to win a stuffed bear; all populated by happy children and weary but equally happy parents.

Once, it must have been the July Fourth after my freshman high school year, I came upon a carnival booth selling ride tickets and it was being manned by my Spanish teacher. I felt a quick embarrassment on his behalf because I was old enough by then to know instinctively what that meant: teachers were insufficiently paid, and had to seek bits of additional income anywhere and any way they could be found.

For a long time there was also a Fourth of July parade in our town. The most thrilling feature for me was the high school band marching at its head and, if one were lucky, playing a Sousa march as it passed your spot. By the time I got to my own five years as a member of that band (I was needed early, in eighth grade, because of a shortage in the percussion ranks) the Fourth of July parades had been pretty much lost to history and we had to be content with marching in the much less festive Memorial Day parade to the town cemetery.

The fourth of July parade might include a few tractors or other farm implements (hey, we're in Iowa, remember?), some marching military veterans, some vintage automobiles, maybe the current high school homecoming queen and her court, maybe some local politicians, and in the early days maybe a couple of floats an organization had gone to some effort to construct.

My proud one-time contribution to this tradition came when I decided our church young folks group should contribute a float. The design and theme were pretty mundane—a church with steeple and the words "Freedom of Religion" on the side. Actually my father built the thing and stretched the chicken wire to cover it; I was left with only the task of stuffing variously colored paper napkins into the chicken wire. So this 'church' riding behind a tractor gave its contribution to one year's parade. We won some kind of prize—second or third place, as I recall, which slightly annoyed me because I thought it was the best thing in the parade and it was, I believe, possibly the only 'float' that year.

We still have a big reminder of Iowa Fourth of July parades in our New England home, an oversized original oil painting hanging in the main staircase showing the beginning of the high school band marching down main street in Harlan. It's the work of the Iowa artist James Polzois who grew up in Harlan, although it was executed in Charleston where he spent most of his working career and where he became a treasured friend during our decade of splitting the year between Charleston and Hartford.

Parades in the Midwest always made a big impact, however, when a town turned one hundred years old it was a very special event. There were a cluster of such towns about the time Winterset celebrated its own centennial, usually a few years hence since Winterset was one of the older Iowa county seat towns. In fact, the centennial parade was usually the main feature of these landmark events.

The Winterset centennial parade, during my perhaps second grade year, was a big, long, splashy, exuberant affair, with lots of high school bands from surrounding towns and a plethora of actual floats in which organizations and businesses had actually invested time and money (as well as assorted delivery vans carrying the names of businesses which had not exerted the time or contributed the money needed for a float). I've never witnessed a better parade in person, although any Rose Bowl parade on television could have given us some stiff competition.

My dad and his machine shop business then-partner created what I was sure was a masterpiece float, and it was driven in the parade on top of a long flat industrial trailer. Atop had been created a perfect "village blacksmith" scene: small children sitting on a grassy slope, watching a (real) blacksmith under his own "spreading chestnut tree" hammering a (real) orange glowing plowshare on a (real) anvil next to his (real) fiery furnace, glowing with (real) flames as he sent his (real) sparks into the air.

# July

It's a wonder the thing didn't go up in flames before the end of the parade. But I was just a small boy who didn't know much of anything yet, and I was super proud of my dad for making this tremendous contribution to what surely must have been the greatest parade ever (and almost certainly the greatest parade ever in Winterset).

Some years down the road in high school, I got to march as a member of the Winterset H.S. Band in the centennial parade of my birthplace town of Greenfield, next county over. Of course I got to see none of the parade, being stuck in the middle of it, but it must have been a red letter day for Greenfield. There had been a lively scramble for the best perches from which to watch, and my grandfather was able to get my parents seats on the front porch of the house of his business partner in the town's Esso gas station. Everyone seemed excited and full of civic pride; a Norman Rockwell picture of America in its most innocent and robust splendor.

Any Iowa town with a college or university, of which there were many, got a bonus in the parade department at homecoming time. I have a vivid memory from about second grade of spray painted young men wearing just little loin cloths, courtesy of one of the great annual parades in the state. Who, after all, had seen silver people before? Iowa State College (now University) where my dad had worked during the war, staged an annual celebration called "Veishea" which featured perhaps the most elaborate student organized parade in the state; certainly more elaborate than the homecoming parades I experienced at Wartburg or at (I hate to admit) my beloved University of Iowa.

The Veishea parade was so good that it lured my dad back to Ames for several years after he'd moved his young family to Winterset. The year I got to go along on this pilgrimage featured a float on which a number of students had painted themselves a glistening silver and had arranged themselves in some kind of classical tableau. My dad explained to me that covering one's entire body with paint would/could be fatal, and that the students had to leave a patch of skin near the base of their spines unpainted in order for the skin to breath. That seemed to explain why the guys wore silver loin cloths; in order not to ruin the illusion that they were totally sliver. The girls had an easier job in hiding their patch of open skin in that they wore flowing silver-painted robes under their silver heads and arms.

Of course, Fourth of July in Winterset, as in cities and towns across the country then, meant fireworks in the evening; and they were never postponed to another day because the fourth didn't happen to fall on a weekend, as is so disconcertingly likely to happen now. These were staged by professionals hired for the occasion by the town, but throughout the day and into the evening there was also the happy din of explosions from private fireworks caches and offered into the mix by the solid citizen patriots who also had made sure their homes displayed a lot of red, white, and blue for the day.

Private fireworks must have been illegal in Iowa in those days (but no cop would even think of tracking down or harassing an offender on the Fourth of July) because I remember that anyone going south of the border into Missouri was expected to bring home fireworks. If you were friendly with one of the livestock truckers in town, you gave him money to bring back fireworks for the Fourth, as well as oleo margarine which must also have been illegal in Iowa. Then one sat around massaging the plastic pouch the oleo came in, trying to distribute evenly the dot of orange food coloring to make the stuff look more like butter, and waiting for the next patriotic opportunity to use the fireworks.

The most elaborate fireworks my dad ever allowed were fairly simple rockets which produced a few flashes of light at their apex but were mostly for noise it seemed. For the most part we played with simple firecrackers and sparklers. The sparklers could be waved around by hand to produce whatever patterns intrigued us, or stuck in the ground in rows or patterns. Firecrackers could simply be lit and tossed, although I developed the habit of sticking them in the end of the hollow iron crossbar of Mom's clothesline poles where they produced a satisfactory flash of fire and a much louder report.

More elaborate fireworks on a private level were an occasional part of the scene, too, but not particularly on the Fourth of July. One of my dad's uncles always brought out a treat for us boys whenever we would visit his new retirement house on the edge of the land he had farmed during his working years. The treat was a little display of several rockets shot off into the night air which exploded into oceans of wild colors and swooping lights. Uncle August's fireworks had traveled through Missouri to reach us too, as it seemed any private fireworks in Iowa had.

On holidays which were not the sacred Fourth of July, the schedule was a bit less formulaic. Mostly my memory is that my dad would take a friend, or a visiting relative, or even me at times, out fishing on the town lake. He had built himself a row boat from scratch, and not just a skimpy little one either, (I'm pretty sure there was no 'Kit' involved in the project), as well as a steel trailer upon which to haul it around behind the family sedan.

This always seemed to provide him with joy. When he took me along, I can remember mostly silence and calm. He and whomever was with him would just float around the lake keeping their thoughts to themselves and enjoying a sort of undemanding male companionship which they seem to have craved.

# July

Once when I had been invited into this masculine secret den, we were floating around on the lake's surface as usual in a very quiet, very calm, very uneventful peace. The older guys had caught a fish or two, but I had snagged nothing, which bothered me not a whit—it did not even seem to be the actual point of the exercise.

Suddenly, breaking the calm dramatically, a relatively large fish jumped out of the water and directly into my lap. It flopped around for a time, apparently as surprised as was I. Everyone had a little laugh and then my dad added my fish to the stringer of catch, and we resumed the peaceful experience for which we had come. I had once again required divine intervention (or at least that of Mother Nature) to become sort of just 'one of the boys.'

Of other national holidays, Winterset made the most of Memorial Day, but left Labor Day totally for individual families to figure out—usually with a picnic, if anything out of the ordinary. Memorial Day, however, brought lots of folks out to the cemetery to place freshly picked flowers on family graves; it was also widely called "Decoration Day." Memorial Day also involved a parade composed of veterans marching in their old uniforms (or whatever parts still fit the man; at least a hat), Boy Scouts, and the high school band, all marching through town on the way to the local cemetery for a brief ritual honoring those who had given their lives in various wars and national conflicts.

This parade on Memorial Day was always routed past a modest little square (actually just a quarter of a standard town block) which functioned as our third official park (after the town's park, which was always referred to as the "City" park, and the nearby state park). This "Memorial Park" vest pocket square gave Winterset a little touch of Parisian extravagance despite its somber job description—to remind us of those from our midst who had sacrificed themselves in the Civil War, and by extension in the two great wars and several conflicts which had demanded blood from Winterset just as they had from small towns around the country.

At the center of the Memorial Park (later renamed, curiously, "Monumental Park," which seemed to vastly overstate its miniscule size) was a tall stone pillar on a platform of native limestone. This local version of an obelisk was attended in four directions by civil war cannons with giant wheels and piles of cannon balls fixed into little pyramids. There was usually a wreath placed on the base of the central column on Memorial Day and before I was old enough to march as a Boy Scout, or later in the high school band, the little park served as my almost private reviewing stand for the parade. The majestic Elms which towered over the park in my day eventually fell victims to a disease which removed the green umbrella from the whole town, and left it feeling a lot less like Paris and a lot more like Dodge City.

Although we were still a long way from the now popular Covered Bridge Days festival, there did seem to be various special days sprinkled around the calendar. Mostly, these were events contrived by the town merchants. The sidewalks of the Square would be lined with racks and tables of merchandise. Mostly, I suspect, this was stuff which had not sold well inside the stores and thus was held back for these sidewalk extravaganzas, probably marked down in price a bit. Maybe that's just cynicism from old age, however. My sister-in-law remembers the street merchandise as new and wonderful stuff which had never before been offered by the stores.

As a smaller child I loved July especially because the evenings were so long; almost another whole play day after dinner. Daylight Savings Time was a manmade manipulation of light which some adults felt was a violation of nature, or perhaps an affront to God who evidently had assigned certain events to their places on the clock, and presumably had dictated the numbering of the hours as well.

Children were free not to contemplate such deep concerns, so they instead reveled in the extra light of the long evenings, a light so unique one could hardly think of an apt comparison from any other time of year. After school started again, October sometimes offered something almost comparable but this time it was a gift of nature rather than man. Indian summer days, those rare God-send miracles of happy delusion offered the same light, but in the late afternoon rather than the late evening. ⌘

# 8 August
## Fair Time

Every mid-to-late summer, there was the county fair held on its own grounds at the edge of town and providing the culminating highlight of summer in Winterset. This was timed to run before the deservedly famous Iowa State Fair so that the 4-H kids could take their prize-winning livestock on to the next level of competition. After a summer of routine play or work, the county fair was a welcome, almost exotic, diversion. Even as relatively young children we were allowed to spend as much time as we wanted at the fair, and we could ride our bikes out to the fairgrounds in complete confidence that the bikes would still be there to take us home when we were ready to give up for the day.

County fair meant another visiting carnival to provide the "Mid-Way," plus food stands offering indulgent but probably unhealthy treats, barns full of animals being judged, lots of jams and other canned goods competing for ribbons along with arrangements of fresh flowers from local gardens, pumpkins and decorative gourds of sometimes surprising girth, and other attractions I've probably forgotten but enjoyed enthusiastically at the time. The fair always seemed like holiday time, and since my parents didn't have the budget to take travel vacations every year the fairs filled in as a welcome substitute toward the end of each summer, giving us a little inexpensive excitement before another school year clipped our wings. The Madison County fair grounds were not all that large back then, and the shows not all that exotic, but in the eyes of school children it was the stuff of wonder and high adventure.

There was also at every county fair an evening show under lights which more often than not was some kind of jalopy race or demolition derby. One year my friend Keith and I were recruited to sell souvenirs to the mostly men watching this spectacle of destruction. "Buy a county fair pennant; prove to the wife you were here tonight!" Keith yelled to the crowd. Wow. We were still mere lads but a hint of worldliness was beginning to edge its way into our world-view.

I'd often have the chance while growing up also to sample the Adair County fair next county over because I'd be visiting my grandparents there. We kids, my brother and I, had latched on to the term "summer vacation," and our parents would oblige by sending us twenty miles away to stay for a few days with my mother's parents, for minimal investment of scarce money.

Grandma would give us chores to do for a dollar or so which gave us pocket money. She would take us fishing, which was her primary indulgence it seemed. We had our own little apartment on the second floor of my grandparents' house where I'd been born and where my uncle and his new bride had lived years previously, although the space was now unfurnished and we had to sleep on the floor on a blanket. This small inconvenience did not seem to hurt our young bones at all. We'd go to the Methodist church on Sundays with our grandfather—Grandma had declared her independence from that ritual many years previously.

These 'vacations' did the job pretty well for years, but the attraction started to fade with increasing age. One year when I was starting to crave a wider engagement with the world, I decided I would buy a *Time* magazine to savor during my Greenfield holiday (or maybe 'exile' as these periods were beginning to feel). I tried the drug stores on the town square first, then grocery stores, then I found myself walking everywhere in town on this quest, stopping even at every gas station. *Time* was simply not to be found in Greenfield—in fact, I don't recall finding any periodicals remotely in that league; maybe journals of any description were not available retail in the town.

And, Grandma would always take us to the county fair for a day. Adair was a smaller county in population than Madison County, and therefore staged a smaller fair, but it did have a larger, and covered, audience amphitheater for its shows (compared to just open air bleachers at home in Madison County). This county fairground had an intriguing ghost story attached, and my elders would recount it on many an evening as they sat around perhaps playing "table-up."

It seems that this Adair County Fair ground's amphitheater was haunted, or perhaps that at least some folks liked the idea that it was. Many people in the county, including my father, had observed a light crossing back-and-forth in this amphitheater like someone carrying a lantern and running back and forth the length of the structure. These observations were not from fair time; they were from any time of year at all. The locals took it seriously, although they did not know what to make of it. Some proposed that it as a weird electrical phenomenon, perhaps a fire-ball trapped and bouncing from end-to-end of the amphitheater. Oddly, though, I never heard of anyone who actually tried to investigate the phenomenon. Maybe it had its greatest value as folklore, and the locals did not want to risk the loss of good gossip for mere scientific evidence.

This recollection of the mysterious lights at the Adair County Fairground was often recounted by my elders, as I've mentioned, as they played "table-up." For this game they would sit around a card-table and place their hands palm-down on its top surface while repeating "table-up, table-up" in rhythmic sequence. Eventually, sure enough, the table would rise a few inches off the floor and would remain suspended so long as everyone kept their hands on the table and kept chanting. As you will well imagine, I was totally fascinated by this as a small boy, just as I have never outgrown my curiosity about the Adair County Fair amphitheater or the many other stories of mysterious manifestations my elders told each other as I tried to memorize their stories.

To mention county fairs and omit mention of the great Iowa State Fair would be inexcusable. State Fair was something of a holy experience for Iowans. No matter where one lived in Iowa, during fair time you were either in Des Moines or wishing you were there.

My brother and I as small kids were not allowed to go to Des Moines with our parents for their annual pilgrimage, but it was a much anticipated annual event nonetheless. Our mother would get two shopping bags from one of the many exhibitors in the "Varied Industries" exhibition building, and stuff them with all kinds of promotional give-aways as she toured this large building. When our parents returned we boys each had this wonderful grab bag full of all kinds of interesting things to play with: pens, rulers, notebooks, buttons and badges, toys, things both practical and fanciful.

When finally we were old enough to go to State Fair ourselves the trip was easily the highlight of the year. We had to get up really early that day, but the anticipation made it worth the sacrifice. Local residents near the fairgrounds would give over their front yards to parking by fair-goers for a few extra bucks in the annual budget, and our dad had his favorite parking host with whom he'd always exchange a few words as if they were old friends. Then we'd walk a couple or three blocks to the grand entrance to the fairgrounds, in my day a big display of neon featuring depictions of huge ears of Iowa corn.

Inside the gates was awaiting a wonderland offering many acres of fascination and joy for young boys, and for anyone lucky enough to be there. The heart of the place, the many open barns for the judging of farm livestock specimens, was only of minor interest to me, a "city" kid, after all. I did take a step into another world every year at the fair, though, watching with fascination the farm kids who dozed with their animals in the stalls, or groomed them for the judges. I did find the exhibition of wild prairie animals worthwhile, and of course, like all who came to the fair, a moment of homage to the famous "butter cow" was absolutely obligatory. Some other states may have also had butter sculptures on display at their state fairs, we were told, but leave it to Iowa to hit the nail squarely on its head: a butter cow.

My favorite part of the state fair always turned out to be wandering around the "Varied Industries Building", where our mother had gathered fair souvenirs for us when we were younger. The promotional swag given away at these booths caught my imagination and never really let go. As an adult running my own business, my secret joy at trade shows and conventions was always having plenty of swag to hand out, whether it made economic sense or not.

How does one fairly describe such an extravagant event as the Iowa State Fair? It truly deserved its reputation as one of the country's largest and finest. Our long days as fair goers were always stuffed with adventure after adventure.

And, not to be ignored, was the food. Some of my mother's relatives put up a food tent each year, so that would be our basic lunch stop. Fair food was anything but *haute cuisine*. It was instead appealing for its sheer capitulation to man's craving for grease and sugar. Fair food was meant for fun as much as, or maybe even more than, for nutrition. Eating like that at any other time of year would have produced deep guilt in the adults. State Fair, however, was a pass; a brief excursion into sheer self-indulgence.

When we were old enough to walk around the fair on our own, one of my happy rituals was going to the television studio building to be part of the audience for live broadcasts. TV was still relatively a new thing, and local stations created lots of shows to be broadcast live from their own studios rather than the much heavier dependence on network fare we know today. So, a special building was constructed on the fair ground with several studios where people could watch live broadcasts by local celebrities.

This was not yet the day of small highly portable video cameras, but the day of the big clunker machines rolling around on heavy bases with a cameraman behind each one. Television broadcasters therefore needed real estate at the fair ground to broadcast remotely. One year when our cousin Jimmy was visiting at fair time, I sat proudly next to him high up in the audience for the "Mary Jane Chin Show" (KRNT? WHO? Can't remember that much detail) when Jimmy won something because of hailing from the farthest distance (Buffalo, New York) in that particular audience. TV no longer needing such heavy equipment, and local TV having been pretty much reduced to news broadcasts, the television building is now used for home cooking demonstrations and other such less exciting audience events.

Each long fair day was climaxed by attending the big evening show at the large amphitheater. I got the impression tickets were relatively expensive for the time, but it was an indulgence my father never denied himself, or us. Whatever show was on the card that night, the evening always ended with a lavish fireworks display. Then we'd head back to Winterset, we boys usually falling asleep during the return trip.

Fairs were inherently wholesome, at least if one discounted the food. They honored the bounty of nature and the hard work of those who harnessed it to provide food for humanity. But they also sometimes took little detours into less honorable human instincts which only catered to our wish for amusement. From my first school boy visit to the state fair I was intrigued by the animals not in the livestock barns, but sold out in the open avenues of the crowded grounds. Mostly these seemed to be reptiles, such as the tiny lizards affixed to chains and worn by both women and men who pinned them to their shirts or caps. This trade seemed exploitative even to a small kid like me, but I could be drawn into the web myself. One of my fair souvenirs was a very small turtle, who then lived in my mother's kitchen in a little plastic water dish for years.

For years, that is, until my dad got the idea that the turtle would be happier in a larger environment. He found an old iron kettle and rigged it up to hang on a clothesline post. We put in some water plants from the dime store, meant for fish tanks, and set my turtle free into his new almost vast universe. Unfortunately as the summer heated up, the sun turned the whole experiment into a kettle of turtle soup.

These county and state fairs were a celebration of how we Iowans fed ourselves (as well as large parts of the world, and not with turtle soup), and a reminder that although most Iowans now live in towns and cities (which was beginning to be the case even back then), none of us were far removed from the farm with its ethic of self-reliance. In a way, our fairs, county or state, were all about food. And not only the indulgent fair-type food with its fatty or sugary extravagance which sent health concerns off on a temporary vacation, but our every-day food. Images of the fairs revolve around 4-H kids grooming, and often sleeping overnight with their animals, or the rows of displayed garden produce, vases of arranged flowers, and canned food bedecked with prize ribbons.

I was never a farm boy, my closest experience having been visits to my dad's parents before they retired from farm life, and I always thought of myself as a city kid despite the smallness of Winterset. But if you were an Iowan, the farm always loomed big no matter where you lived, and a certain agricultural aura influenced everything. Iowans didn't just live on, and off of, the land; we were almost organically *of* the land in a mystical way.

The first students at my beloved University of Iowa were given the chance to pick the school colors, and they chose black and gold—black for the rich Iowa soil which gave life and identity and livelihood to the plains. To drive across the Mississippi and catch the first glimpse of that incredibly black Iowa soil remains one of life's joyous little pleasures for me.

So, Iowans tend to be gardeners, writ either large or small. We are either farmers by profession, or gardeners by avocation; there seems to be no other choice, nor would we want there to be. After moving to town in retirement or living in town a generation or two after one's people left the land, having a garden was part of the unquestioned Iowa way of life. In town flowers may have claimed more of the garden space than they did on the farm, but the main work of the garden was still to produce food. Most in-town properties had working gardens (although a few "grand" West End gardens may have reverted to flowers or kitchen gardens only) which actually contributed significantly to the household larder. Iowans love the land, and Iowans love to be practical.

If one did not have sufficient space for a garden, one at least planted one or two fruit trees, or rented land for a garden from a neighbor. An etched-in summer memory for me was helping my mother pick strawberries from the large garden her parents always rented and planted with row after row of the delectable fruit. When I'd go across the street in Winterset to visit my dad's parents, I'd marvel at the huge pile of potatoes, home-grown in a garden that covered half the property, now harvested and heaped under the stairs down to the basement, awaiting mashing for winter dinners.

Anyone from my era who grew up in Iowa will have memories of a mother or grandmother canning home-grown vegetables and fruit. The steaming kitchen then gave way to rows and rows of glass jars stored in the basement against the encroaching winter.

This agricultural milieu pervaded Iowa life even for us "urban" types. High School had a large 4-H club which met weekly after hours. It seemed alien to me although always a point of some curiosity. What could these farmer kids do or talk about sitting around a school classroom? They could have been practicing Satanic rituals for all I knew. But later when my parents went through a brief period planning to buy and move to a farm, my first thought was, "Now I'm going to have to join 4-H," although I was still not sure exactly what it was all about.

Yes, we had grocery stores way back then, of course. But while they were handy, and increasingly relied upon, relying on oneself was the Iowa way and that applied to food as much as to anything else. What's more, we were not all that far removed from the scarcity of the war years, and Iowans had learned their lesson. The "Victory Gardens" had not faded from adult memory, nor yet either as a practicality of life.

In my day a lot of folks described even Des Moines as just an overgrown country town. All of our lives, be we rural or city people, were permeated with agriculture and our attachment to the rich Iowa soil. Now, years later, Des Moines is still a symbol of this connection to the land. She may have been known for a time to the rest of the country for the early politics of the nation's presidential nominating process, but she is equally still a celebration of food and the agriculture that provides it. Tourists, and just plain Iowans, flock to the state fair, to the world headquarters and museum of a major world food prize, to the "Living History Farm" reconstruction park, and to the weekly summer plenitude of one of the most famous farmers' markets in the country.

Maybe this orientation to food, and its production, was the explanation for the popularity of pot-luck dining in Iowa. Of course, during my school days there were not all than many restaurants available for social dining. But our love of pot-luck dinners went beyond necessity; there was a do-it-yourself quality to them which appealed to the Iowa ethos. They were part of the glue which held churches and social clubs together.

My grandest pot-luck memories are of the annual Drake family reunions, always offering a grand spread of home-made food and held on a lovely limestone block farm house front yard near Greenfield (my mother's family included Drakes in some way I never really figured out, except to realize we might have had a connection with the founders of Drake University in Des Moines). Pot-luck dinners were simply the *de facto* heart of family reunions and family holidays. They brought friends together and introduced new friends. Even a dinner by invitation was slightly turned into a pot-luck because in Iowa then one always brought along a dish to contribute to the table; bringing a bottle of wine was something easterners might do, but in Iowa one brought a salad or a casserole.

For a short period of time late summer brought other outdoor entertainment as well, not quite up to fair standards but making a vaguely similar contribution. In the early period of my Winterset school days a large open air (roof only) auditorium stood behind the Methodist church, about a block from my house. It was called "Chautauqua" although I think that term might more accurately be applied to the "shows" it hosted during the summer which consisted mostly of traveling preachers and revivalists; a sort of early and miniature version of the Billy Graham 'crusades' which would captivate religious folks a few years down the road. This tradition had as its inspiration the Chautauqua annual camp ground gathering in New York, and various other similar religious-oriented camp grounds around the east, such as that at Ocean Grove in New Jersey. The Winterset version of this tradition was already dying during my early school days, and before long the Chautauqua amphitheater was torn down and replaced by a couple new family houses.

The religiosity of our little Chautauqua was balanced out most summers when travelling tent shows would set up in town for a few nights' run. These offered as entertainment rather raunchy skits of men and women carrying on in various 'R' rated slapstick ways, with some decidedly non-classical music thrown into the mix. I know this only because local boys could get free tickets by helping to unload the folding chairs from the show's trucks, and then setting them up under the big tent for the anticipated audience. None of the adults in my family were ever interested in sharing my tickets, but I would venture over to the tent alone to soak up some culture. Today, I'd not be surprised if such shows would impose a minimum age for audience members, assuming they still exist at all. ⌘

# 9 September Sleep-Overs

It was the legendary first day of school. I was standing in this strange room which was about to lay claim to me, and not sure what my reaction was supposed to be. My mother stood next to me and we watched the other couples, mothers each with a subdued, apprehensive child, standing around the room awaiting something. I didn't really understand what this something was, but I had gotten the message that it was going to radically alter my life; I was going to be taken captive along with lots of other innocent little kids my age. Many of the kids were softly crying. Taking my social clues from my fellow short people, I decided maybe the appropriate thing to do was to cry—after all, no one seemed to be offering any alternative plan of action.

"Don't cry, look, there's Bobby over there," comforted my mother pointing to my first little friend from the neighborhood. Oh, okay, so crying was not the expected reaction then either. Please explain to me what my role is here.

Finally a woman I'd never seen before started talking and seemed to have some kind of authority. Thank God—I didn't especially care what she was saying, but someone was clearly needed to take charge of this weird scene. She hadn't talked for very long when the mothers began to leave. Okay, progress of some sort was being made. I didn't have to cry to impress my mother any longer, having already registered my lack of total enthusiasm for this developing new arrangement. I was now free to join the other little kids so that we could pool our collective resources and try to get to the bottom of things.

All of a sudden we had been gathered around a piano and our formal educations had begun—the very first small step in what would become many years of school classes; for me twenty years' worth. Well, at least we were now officially scholars, whatever that might mean. So we sat on the floor learning and singing the Kindergarten anthem (or was it the Kindergarten fight song?): "Little Ducky Duddle."

"Little Ducky Duddle / Went wadding in a puddle / Went wadding in a puddle quite small / Said he 'it doesn't matter / How much I splash and splatter / I'm only a ducky, after all.'" It's wonderful how the masterpieces stay with one's memory for life, even when lesser things begin to fade.

If there was any residual apprehension for the next few days, it faded completely, and my life significantly changed, with the acquisition of a playmate who would later become my university roommate and life-long friend.

Doug was a bit late in joining our Kindergarten class, because he and his mother had just moved to Winterset to live with her father. He was a retired shoe store operator from the Square, now a widower, house-bound, and dependent on assistance. At any rate, the Kindergarten teacher, whether out of an attempt to bridge my shyness or maybe just arbitrarily, I can only wonder, appointed me to shepherd the new boy around the halls which I hardly knew yet myself.

My first big assignment was to show him where to pee.

There was a ritual each day where everyone had to form two lines, with the boys marching single file to the "Men's" and the girls to the "Ladies'." These rooms were located, dungeon-like, in the deep bowels of the building. I'm not sure I ever actually peed on these expeditions, being as shy as I was and because they took place at arbitrary times. But we did dutifully march and did dutifully place ourselves for the allotted time in front of a urinal.

After marching single file back to our class room, we could then resume the intellectual or musical education upon which we'd embarked. Doug and I would sit, or nap, next to each other whenever there was a logistical option, and when the final bell for the day rang we often continued our exploration of the greater world together.

Somewhat more into the ascending hierarchy of school grades, Doug's mother decided to form a Cub Scout pack. I was at his house most of the time anyway, so of course I joined up.

Now a uniformed man, the door was opened for me to march in lots of parades and otherwise practice being what they called a "solid citizen." Mostly, however, we made belts for our fathers for Fathers' Day, wove lanyards out of plastic strips to hold lord-knows-what necessities around our necks, and hiked in the woods. On one of these hiking occasions the urgently clear voice of our Den Mother (Doug's mom) rang out "**rattlesnake**!" I had straggled from the group and so didn't know exactly where said rattlesnake was; my only option was to freeze in place for a moment and then carefully, very carefully, try to rejoin my pack.

## September

Cub Scouts, vanilla flavored though it normally was, also became the stage for one of the most humiliating, yet revelatory, little vignettes of my childhood.

At one scout meeting Doug's mom decided we would play a game where two of us would be sent out in advance, and the balance of boys along with our Den Mother would come along a bit later and try to track the first two from their chalk marks left on sidewalks. The rules were that if the two did anything but walk straight forward, a mark was to be left at that point to indicate the new route. I guess the point was to develop skills in us as observant trackers, or maybe just to encourage the purchase of chalk from local stores.

I was chosen to be one of the advance team, the markers, and my partner was, well, I don't recall his name but he was one of the popular kids in school and, I thought, rather authoritative and sure of himself. I wanted to be his friend, and although he had hardly noticed me previously, here I was partnered with him—do you think a little matter like honesty or personal integrity was going to make me disobey any word which issued from his popular mouth?

So, he came up with the brilliant and scallywag idea that we would turn right, but chalk that we had turned left; a simple flouting of the rules requiring not much intelligence but demonstrating an air of appealing security. My good boy inclinations tried to reject such an obvious breach of Cub Scout uprightness but they were smothered utterly by my need to be liked by this boy. So we chalked in the other direction and then went back to Doug's place and hid in the big old barn on the property. I'm sure my partner in crime thought it would be the greatest hoot, and the greatest surprise when the others finally found us.

When the search group came back, the Den Mother announced with a bit of unchecked indignation that they had seen us make the maneuver but had turned in the direction of the chalk mark anyway in a display of Cub Scout integrity.

I really was disgusted with myself for failing to uphold my own integrity and to be now diminished in the eyes of Doug's mom, but I also had a sort of thrill in standing shoulder-to-shoulder in solidarity with the popular boy and sharing equally in his humiliation—and hoping that we'd henceforth be friends. We were not henceforth any closer to being friends than we had ever been; my investment of lost honor having paid no dividends.

That barn actually played a significant role for me during grade school.

Doug's house was a sizeable Victorian with turrets, little open step-out balcony-like spaces, a big twisting front hall staircase, and all manner of detail which I found utterly charming. My house, by contrast, was a very simple, not large, utilitarian and plain structure of the "farmhouse" variety, as the local language would have it.

Naturally, I spent as much time at Doug's place as I could get by with, including a number of chatty sleep-overs. The place and house were likely not as grand nor as large as they seemed at the time through the eyes of a mere lad, but the property was large enough that it now hosts two family homes, the original and a much later one built after Doug's family moved on. This johnny-come-lately house represents what I guess I would call the "Suburban" style, i.e. not any more interesting than the "farmhouse" variety.

Doug and his mother were in that lovely old Victorian place because her father needed care (it was somewhat before the nursing home craze hit town, and families still took care of their own). It was also before commuting long distances to work became commonplace, so Doug's father had just rented a room near his job in Des Moines and accepted the weekend limitations that placed on family life.

Doug's grandpa died when we were in seventh or eighth grade, setting the stage for Doug to make it only part way through high school in Winterset. Doug was not in school for a day or so after his grandfather died. "What a brave boy you have been," said our math teacher when he showed up in class again; even then it had a rather condescending ring to it, but it was true, I suppose, that for most of us any encounter with death was still mostly at least a few years in the future.

For me that first encounter came in high school when I lost a grandmother. But then it picked up steam and stated in no uncertain terms that it would be a major player; hogging for itself a leading role in the story just beginning to unfold otherwise with so much promise and potential. And it made abundantly clear that death was not reserved just for old folks. Shortly after high school I had to deal with the discomfort of hearing that Betty, my sixth grade quasi-girlfriend, had died shortly after her marriage.

Two years later at university I was happily reading the *Des Moines Register* when I noticed a small article on a death in Winterset. Keith, my childhood friend of so many years and so many adventures had been killed when a grain storage bin he had been working near exploded in the autumn heat. While trying to flee the avalanche he tripped over a piece of equipment and was buried in corn. No, young and optimistic though we may have been, none of us were going to escape the repercussions of the dark stranger who had been in our midst all along.

But back to Doug and back to the happy innocence of childhood. On this large double lot, beside the house and a large garden and big open front yard, was the old two-full-storied barn I've been telling you about. The barn served as a garage on the first level, but on the second level and outside to its back and side it served as Doug's small private kingdom.

It was in Doug's big old barn that he and I at another time planned to stage our own circus. We practiced doing what we thought were circus-like things for hours in the barn, but made extremely little progress in coming up with a plan which could compete with Ringling Brothers.

One of the 'acts' we were working on one day found Doug running around in his long underwear and no trousers. I wish I could remember what we thought this was supposed to lead to, or why we thought people would want to pay money to watch it.

Anyway, improvising circus acts as we went along, I grabbed an umbrella and started pursuing him. I extended the crook handle of the umbrella and caught the back of his long-johns' waist. This set the stage for the most overt sexual experience of my Winterset elementary grade school days—I caught a glimpse of his bare bottom.

Not a big glimpse, but some skin in any case. I was a little confused about how I was supposed to react; to continue the game, to expose more flesh, to apologize, to be ashamed? We abandoned whatever idea for a circus act it was supposed to have been. Doug merely said, "Don't tell Momma."

It surprises me, actually, that there was never anything else about which Momma should not have been told.

Doug and I spent lots of time in his room, but I recall no lack of clothing, no sex talk, nothing that boys (straight or otherwise) are universally thought to do or talk about between themselves as adolescents.

Then there were the equally Sunday-School-pure sleep overs I've mentioned, in the double bed of the upstairs guest room. The pajamas always stayed on, and the most risqué talk I can remember was stuff like, "Did you know Craig was adopted?" This kind of information sharing felt rather intimate in and of itself.

An exciting event in Winterset at that time was the opening of a new grocery store at the edge of town. A local big-wig was developing a whole little neighborhood of several businesses, including a bowling alley which contained the only real restaurant in town, at least if one measured by big town standards. He had just built and opened the "Biz-Mart," a grocery store, and the building featured an exotic 'first' for Winterset—doors that opened automatically at the approach of a patron. People were fascinated, and would sometimes take visitors to the Biz-Mart just to show off these sliding doors.

During one of those nights in Doug's guest bedroom I learned that the preacher at the local Presbyterian church (to which Doug's family belonged not surprisingly, being of Scottish heritage) had said in a Sunday sermon that when we got to Heaven the "gates would swing open just like the doors at the Biz-Mart."

Well, Craig's dad, one of my future employers, owned a grocery store on the Square which had conventional doors. I learned during this particular night of boyish gossip that Craig's dad was infuriated at the preacher's reference, and boycotted the Presbyterian Church thereafter. Such was the intrigue and drama of small town life, and such was the gossip shared at sleep-overs—at least between Doug and me.

Even then, and even with me being little Mr. Goody-Two-Shoes, I recall being vaguely aware that these sleep-overs could have been opportunities for something more—something that most boys would just do without much concern or forethought, and certainly with no regret. But this awareness was only a hazy something in the very back of my brain, and besides neither Doug nor I at that point would have voluntarily done anything of which momma would not approve—neither his momma nor mine. We were good boys. Actually, maybe more than that; we were engulfed in an age of innocence and in a place which always tried to remain as innocent as it possibly could. At any rate, Doug and I always upheld the innocence standards expected of us.

By the way, the only circus act which came close to being actually plotted out resulted from my reading of the Sears and Roebuck catalog, a favorite small town late Forties activity. I had noticed some dresses I liked (*Please*, don't even start!) and decided I could create one myself with crepe paper, glue and sparkles.

To give myself credit, I didn't imagine wearing this dazzling creation myself—we needed a girl. So we decided our classmate Jane would be a necessary addition to our one-ring show. I had no idea what she would *do* in our circus, except that she would wear my sparkly dress in a kind of *Cirque du Soleil* extravaganza of color and brilliance. This plan ended without Jane ever knowing she had been recruited to the circus life, or my colorful glittering skirt ever being actually constructed.

## SEX ED, WINTERSET STYLE

A curious feature of our high school years, a bit later, was a mandatory assembly once a week called "Chapel," in which a rotation of Winterset's Protestant clergymen would hold-forth for an hour at a time to the assembled non-Catholic student body.

Despite my religious self-identification and manifest hang-ups, I found this exercise as boring and pointless as did my classmates. Daydream City. Although I could write a short synopsis of the contents of all of my high school classes even now, I have no memory whatsoever of anything that was said during these Chapel assemblies; mostly, I suspect, strings of bland aphorisms and feel-good Hallmark sentiments, or more probable still, diluted rehashes of last Sunday's sermons.

The only real involvement I experienced was on the days my own pastor showed up in the rotation. Then the Lutheran flag was flying and I had something at stake; beside which I genuinely liked the man as a father-figure and felt protective of his reputation with my peers. So I'd sit there shoulder-to-shoulder with fidgeting or dozing schoolmates pulling for every one of his words to be just right and hoping he could avoid any embarrassment in the eyes of his late-teen audience. Today that would be an impossible assignment, but back then we were all co-conspirators in the game of keeping everything pleasant, so the rebels just daydreamed and waited for the end-of-period bell.

The very existence of an enforced religious lecture series in our high school seemed, even to a mere teenager, to flirt with a violation of the church-state division we studied about in government (or was it "civics"?) class. Granted that times were simpler and less contentious all-around then, but still, why bring religion into the classroom? Not many years later the country would actually give serious thought to the pluses or minuses of mandatory prayer in schools, but here we were in Winterset blithely sailing along without a thought in the world that such practices could be anything but wholesome.

There were two reasons for high school 'Chapel' I suspect.

First was simply that Winterset was a homogenous enclave of upright white Christian people who saw themselves as being just the way God intended people to be.

We were almost literally the Republican Party at prayer, to borrow a description usually appropriated to the Episcopal Church. That we could be the slightest bit wrong in any cultural practice or detail was something which would just never have crossed anyone's mind. So the high school Chapel tradition was first of all a confident flexing of our cultural muscles: "Onward Christian Soldiers," Rah-Rah, Go Team.

But there was a second, and primary, reason for this odd intrusion of religion into the classroom, I believe. Winterset did not offer formal sex-education in its school system in any way, shape, or form (unless, perhaps one counted the 4-H club meetings, but that's only raw speculation on my part).

In Junior High we had been told a few things about health and healthy living, and if one read *very* carefully between the lines there was a hint or two about certain 'facts of life.' Yet our civic and educational leaders, as well as our religious leaders, must have pulled their heads out of the sand upon occasion and realized that the town's high school kids were likely thinking about areas of life which were not discussed at ladies' auxiliary meetings. What to do? Ah-ha, let's be sure these kids get a solid grounding in the moral, respectable, and approved way to behave. And who better to tell them to keep their pants zipped than the clergy?

This approach reminds me now of Nancy Reagan's "Just Say No" campaign to end drug abuse decades later. Somehow the message was bound to get through without anyone having to stoop to the undignified role of actually talking about sex directly. So we were constantly pointed to the religious north-star and admonished to be good, ethical, moral, etc. Surely any actual education about sex would not then be needed.

At least I don't remember any direct discussion of sexual morality during these so-called Chapel sessions—but then, like my classmates, I have no doubt, I don't actually remember anything at all which was preached to us during that weekly holy hour. But not remembering cuts in two directions. It also means nothing was said, or preached, which would galvanize the attention of a teenaged boy, so I can be pretty sure none of the unseemly details of sexuality or sexual morality were discussed in so many words. Those we would have remembered.

I suspect it was a system of passing the buck. Parents were not especially keen to tackle the details of sex education, so they hoped the school system would take over the bulk of the work. The schools, on the other hand, had no experience (at that time) or ready curriculum (or stomach) for such a responsibility, so they passed along the job to the community's men of great moral rectitude, the clergy. And the clergy always had God to hide behind. Surely just introducing God into the picture and offering words about morality, ethical behavior, and so forth would get the job done. No real need for the messy details.

Maybe they were right! Only one unplanned (or at least out of wedlock) pregnancy occurred during my high school days in Winterset, at least only one that I knew about. And this being a small town, the approaching blessed event was no secret. My mother took me aside to explain that a girl who was with child by a boy who would do such a thing to her, might well be looking for a replacement "husband," i.e. might be looking for a "good boy" who would make a more suitable husband and ersatz father than would her current boyfriend. In other words, steer clear of her.

Well, I was certainly a 'good boy' and I was by then pretty intrigued by sex in any of its possible social contexts, so I perversely took an interest in this girl who, heretofore, I had hardly noticed. Of course, for me to 'take an interest' in a girl was fairly mild stuff. But I did begin to chat with her a bit, now that she was such an interesting, and worldly, figure in our midst.

I discovered that she was not the only pregnant female in her household; that the family dog would soon give birth as well. Okay, I was a dog lover and a dog pregnancy was much safer territory to talk about. In due course I was invited over to see the newborns.

Sitting in her living room was a heady experience to be sure—did she have designs on me as my mother had seemed to warn? Actually the idea was quite titillating, and I felt rather excited that a girl might look at me as a worthy representative of the male half of our species. But if she saw me that way, she was, as it turned out, totally barking up the wrong tree.

But hey, I got a really cute black puppy out of the deal, so I guess I served some sort of step-dad purpose after all.

So, the Protestant students were being spiritually tended to on school grounds and during school hours. Did that leave the Catholic kids to fend for themselves? Hardly. Every week they would gather in the journalism room to hear the local priest lecture them in probably the same vein to which the Protestant kids were being subjected. Was that the case? I wanted to know, and I thought I could get a story for the school paper (of which I was by then the editor) out of it, so I got permission to skip Chapel one week in order to attend the Roman Catholic version and lift the veil of secrecy.

What I discovered was much more juicy than I could have imagined, although I instinctively knew I could not write about it in the school paper.

The priest welcomed me to the session, but did so in a way which actually alarmed me, and which I suspect embarrassed his charges. He hailed my forthcoming story in the *Husky* because it would at last expose the wretched perception of Catholics in Winterset to be lies. The Catholics, he assured us, were not plotting to overthrow the government. They were not planning to bring tanks into the streets to subvert the American way of life. They were not making plans to have Papal forces invade the United States. In short, we Catholics are not the subversives you Protestants think we are.

Was this man nuts or just short of anything constructive to say that week? He certainly appeared paranoid. It was clear he had suffered the strain of feeling that his tribe had long been gravely misunderstood and maybe even slandered. The seemingly inconsequential occasion of my fairly innocent visit to the Catholic version of "Chapel" had uncorked frustrations and resentments which must have long festered in his soul. I certainly, at age 17 or 18, was not sure what to make of this, except to know that my story had just been turned into mush.

## Winterset In Time

I could not repeat what the priest had said; both Winterset propriety and the school administration would forbid that without question. Later in life I spent time as a professional journalist in the field of religion, but perhaps my most interesting such story had been left unwritten back in high school. ⌘

# 10 October
## The Odor of Burning Leaves

A strong and oddly pleasant persistent Winterset memory is autumn bonfires, and their acrid odor and smoke. Fire could turn up almost anywhere and folks could be pretty casual, and even a bit irresponsible, about it. Burning something, almost anything, was the town way of coping with waste, and air pollution had not yet been invented, at least not yet in Iowa.

In the autumn, one raked dead leaves to the curb and set the piles on fire. This habit lent a fairly pleasant odor to autumn days. Lots of households had large steel drums used to burn garbage in. The odors from these sources were generally less pleasant, although no less Winterset.

My aunt and uncle would periodically take the hair clippings swept from the floor of his barber shop and burn them across the street, creating a neighborhood odor which tilted towards the unpleasant side. Fire was viewed more as a tool than a potential danger. It was simply part of our rural, and self-reliant, way of looking at things.

A couple of school grades later the town experienced one of its truly legendary building fires. I was awakened from sound sleep by the fierce light from that fire blasting through the venetian blinds. My brother and I got up to see what was going on. The burning building was three blocks away but flames were shooting high into the sky and the whole town seemed almost like daytime. There were rumors that the fire was being fed by a wax model of a horse in the second floor of the business (my sister-in-law, a daughter of the owner of that business, says it was actually a wooden horse, just for the record). In any case it was the largest fire I've ever witnessed in person, and the brick walls were beginning to give way and collapse onto the street by the time I arrived as a spectator.

My dad was already at the scene along with many other spectators by the time Richard and I got as near as we were allowed to come. By then our dad had been impressed on the spot into the local volunteer fire fighters and was spraying the burning building with a large hose—although the fire raged uncontrollably despite all the hoses aimed at it. The two-story building was a total loss; just a pile of smoldering bricks by morning. The fire, as you might expect, seemed to be all that was talked about at school the next day.

My dad would live to see his younger son serve Winterset as a fireman, and then for nearly a couple decades as the town's fire chief (see Postscript 2). He would also live to become the father-in-law of the daughter of the burned building's owner.

## PLAYING ALONG: THE WINTERSET THEATRICAL SEASON

My one and only shot at theatrical fame in a long life came in high school senior year when I starred (I presume; at least it was a big part to memorize) in the class play.

This was a fairly standard part of high school life in Iowa at the time, although I think it may actually have been staged a bit on a hit-or-miss schedule at Winterset. Nonetheless, the senior class play at the high school represented a solid half of Winterset's theatrical season, the other half being the annual Lions Club minstrel show. I suppose one could also count the traveling tent shows which sometimes came through in the summer, but they tilted toward the risqué so we'll concentrate on the higher minded offerings.

This Lions Club community highlight somehow induced the upstanding and most prominent men of the town to put on blackface, to try to talk with thick southern accents, and to spend two evenings in public each year cracking lame jokes or, even worse, puns: "I'm taking Judy on a trip to Florida / Are you gunna Tampa with her? / Mi-*am*-i." In those days there wasn't a (real) person of color to be seen until one got to Des Moines, and evidently, I was not the only naïve male in town, either. Not everyone on stage was in blackface, although the exceptions were rare; maybe a guitarist or a banjo player providing a musical interlude. Otherwise, it was a pure dose of exactly the fare which today would bring great embarrassment to the town (I assume).

No one seemed to be in the slightest concerned that these shows might amount to racial mockery or that bad taste was involved to the slightest degree, any more than they were embarrassed to rely on bad puns for amusement. I, who would grow up to become a fairly liberal Democrat, nevertheless found them utterly delightful and would attend both nights on the pretext of reviewing them for the school paper. Of course, I was also a budding theater and opera devotee for whom the choice of theatrical nights out in Winterset was a touch restricted. Well, at least there was always the Iowa Theater on the Square, ready to show us a fairly recent Hollywood movie, or, on Saturday afternoons an oater featuring Winterset's own patron saint John Wayne.

Our senior class play was presided over by the drama teacher, who assigned the roles arbitrarily; no one "tried out" for the play. He had chosen a vehicle called "The Family Nobody Wanted," which was every bit as gooey as the title suggests. Still, it was the hit of the Winterset theatrical season—people couldn't stop talking about it for, well, maybe hours.

I had been tapped to play the role of a clergyman ("Minister" I think the role was labeled, as such a person indeed generically would have been called in Winterset at that time, and across most denominational lines).

Anyway, this minister and his wife kept adopting orphaned children of various ethnic backgrounds. Naturally, there were twists and turns as this mélange of people learned to get along with each other. That's about as much of the gripping plot as I can recall now. The real fun was in the many readings and rehearsals after school hours and the sense of comradery they provided to the cast. And we did "sell out" two nights of a full auditorium, although something in the back of my mind tells me the tickets were actually free.

The high school auditorium consisted of a stage, orchestra seating, and some balcony seating. And that was something of a hurdle. There really were no wings of sufficient size to allow adequate theatrical off stage preparation, so, for example, two girls struggled to apply my makeup while we crouched on the stairs leading to the stage on one side, separated from the audience by only a drape. This also meant only one stage setting was feasible. All the props were furniture borrowed from the actors' homes and left in place during intermission. We got through both acts without mishap and the audience applauded with enough enthusiasm to avoid any embarrassment to the cast. In Winterset at the time that was enough to constitute a hit. We accepted the verdict.

At the first session of drama class after the show closed our teacher asked what reactions we'd heard from friends and family. After a few seconds of silence, a girl at the back of the room, Marsha, offered, "My aunt could not believe how old and mature Phil could act." Another pause while I thought to myself: "Type Casting." I may not have fully understood myself yet, but I certainly was aware that I was, in the lingo of the day, a 'square.' The beginning signs of maturity appealed to the teachers, but not so much to my fellow students.

We even had a cast party after the show closed. Everyone was invited to the basement of Craig's home for a no-alcohol and no-drugs celebration (this was 1959, remember, and Winterset was about as wholesome a place as one could find on a map).

This party gave me another of the few he-man episodes of my high school career, albeit without much of an audience, maybe luckily or maybe unfortunately. The party was already going in the basement when I arrived after getting the final touches of make-up removed. As I entered the kitchen, where I already knew the door to the basement was located, two girls were rounding the corner into an open door—I followed them assuming they were going downstairs.

But it turned out they were going into the bathroom, and they reacted with some shock when I came very close to going in with them. I then found the correct door while thinking, "Hey, this could be good for my reputation if they tell anyone." Yep, Phil the stud strikes again; a rarity to be sure, but a little good press can go a long way. And besides, the town newspaper did not review high school senior class plays, alas, so it would be the only press I might get from the entire endeavor. And I was rather painfully aware, even then, that my image on the masculinity front could use a little boost.

Entertainment in those days was not limited to high school football games and Lyon's Club minstrel shows, of course. We were at the cusp of a national addiction. One by one our living rooms acquired a big piece of furniture devoted to showing black and white images on a smallish electronic tube. And our rooftops acquired elaborate metal contraptions designed to snag these images out of thin air and pipe them down to these pieces of handsome, expensive furniture.

The first programming for this new amazing wonder came from Ames, from Iowa State University and its WOI-TV, a national pioneer in the new craze. It offered programming for only a handful of hours a day at the beginning, but in due course there was a surfeit of choice as TV channel after channel began operations in Des Moines. Some did not last all that long; in fact, some of the new TV networks did not even last all that long. But the American scene was changed permanently, and Iowa along with it.

The early days of TV were the most local surprisingly. Lots of shows originated with local channels in their own studios. There was always an assortment of productions coming out of studios in Des Moines, including the iconic "Iowa Barn Dance Frolic" from WHO-TV. It tried to encapsulate what was distinctive about rural music and social get-togethers on the prairie, and offered lots of spirited banjo and fiddle playing and square dancing, all performed live with lots of background hay bales from a Des Moines TV studio. I was always proud and impressed at how Des Moines seemed to be generating as much live TV as the New York networks.

## October

This local programming also created celebrities who were the toast of Iowa, but unknown elsewhere. Gradually this turf was usurped by the networks, leaving local stations to produce nothing more than local newscasts to precede the network news each evening and then maybe to offer a brief recap at eleven p.m. after which all good Iowans promptly went to bed.

When my dad watched TV no one would have even thought of challenging his choice of fare. Of course, Mom was busy in the kitchen cleaning up from dinner. Of course, there were only two or three channels from which to choose in the first place—and no such thing as cable. And of course we kids were happy enough with Dad's choices in any case. He always opted for comedy if it was available, and his favored diet of Red Skelton or Milton Berle seemed perfect to my brother and me.

During the long summer days I seemed to have the TV to myself as a grade school kid. Mostly I remember "When the Moon comes over the Mountain" and especially "God Bless America" belted out by the sturdy contralto Kate Smith. It all seemed so innocent then, but things were getting increasingly complicated as life went on. Even Kate Smith now stands as an emblem not of patriotism, but of racism.

Although it surely seemed that this new television thing was on its way to replacing radio (and indeed it quickly did in the evenings), radio retained an iron fisted hold on lunchtime. I always walked home during school lunch break and my mother would have WHO on, broadcasting live out of their Des Moines studios and offering the latest crop and live-stock market trading statistics and live music. WHO was one of the nation's "clear channel" radio stations, so listeners as far away as Alaska might well have been sharing our lunch-time entertainment. The music varied little day to day; always a country music singer or two accompanied by a guitarist or a fiddler and crooning through another couple of mushy love songs. But the evening radio I had thrived on as a schoolboy before TV, "Amos and Andy," "The Great Gildersleeve," "Fibber McGee and Molly," could not put up a sufficient fight for life in the face of America's new TV fixation.

Oddly enough, this newfangled television thing also rearranged our living quarters. Most local houses were composed of fairly cozy rooms which had served life on the prairie well for ages. But now there was reason to focus on a smallish screen, and it would seem that some of the men were comfortable with this only at a distance; a distance not comfortably allowed by the previously adequate room dimensions.

Thus I grew up with needing to squeeze around a big chair every time I wanted to go into our living room. My dad had placed his big evening chair in the doorway to the living room, evidently to give him the extra inches he needed to focus comfortably on the TV screen. And oddly enough, it was the same when we visited my mother's parents twenty miles west. Her father had placed an equally big chair in about the same position to the entry to their living room. I think my grandpa's chair stayed resolutely in the doorway the rest of his life. My dad, however, eventually moved into the living room after shifting the TV's location and acquiring a big adjustable lounging chair which reclined to his will. Maybe he was also getting less farsighted.

## THE ADULTS' FAVORITE HOLIDAY

As younger children late October had meant begging neighbors for treats (mostly candy, one hoped, although some health-nut would always drop an apple or an orange into our gaping bags) and building up a supply which would last, well, maybe even a day or so if one were frugal. It was time for what increasingly seems like America's greatest holiday of all: Halloween.

When we were very young our range was restricted to a radius of a town block or so, not as I recall because of parental cautiousness, but because the town seemed so big to us small kids and on this scary night venturing too far from home was itself scary. There was no need for a parent to tag along to monitor the proceedings; this was Winterset, these were neighbors, and it was an article of faith that the kids would return safe and sound with bulging bags of sugar thinly disguised in a variety of unhealthy ways.

No one seemed to mind the hordes of begging little urchins, although in retrospect I have to particularly admire the approach of one elderly woman who lived alone. We always threatened "Trick or Treat," but never had any intention of committing the trick part of the equation (actually it took a few years for me to understand that the "trick" aspect was a threat).

This particular lonely little old lady had long ago decided the trick was for her to commit. So we'd knock on her door expecting another contribution to our stockpile of sugar bombs, only to be told that the treat was inside. We had to sit at table with her and eat a nice bowl of chocolate ice cream, or simply leave empty handed. Naturally, we chose the ice cream, and would sit silently enjoying it while our hostess chatted amiably, mostly to herself.

The Halloween costume syndrome outlasted the sugar collection festivities, and we were expected to arrive in disguise at a school party as late as Junior High School. By then I was getting pretty tired of the whole ritual, and had totally run out of costume ideas. I spent a couple days in agony, and intense consultation with my mother, trying to figure out how to dress for the event. It was my mother who, as usual, offered salvation. She suggested dressing as a robot.

## October

I found a cardboard box just large enough to cover my torso and painted it silver. Then I covered my arms and legs with crunched up aluminum foil. How I covered my face and head I don't quite remember now, but perhaps with another cardboard box. By the time I got to the school party I was feeling a lot better, and more confident. To the best of my memory that last school party costume may have been the best of the lot. Out of desperation had been born success, and I closed out my Halloween years in triumph.

Now I'm the adult, the retired guy who has to respond to the doorbell and hand out generous scoops of candy. I don't find that the most surprising development along Halloween lines, however. What surprises me is how much other American *adults* still seem to love Halloween. It isn't the kids who put up elaborate lawn decorations of witches and jack-o'-lanterns, it's their elders. Somehow I've failed to be part of the majority yet again. I just can't work up the level of enthusiasm that so many adults demonstrate with their fixation on Halloween.

Even as small children it was obvious to us that, in its early weeks, October was in its way the most generous of months. It offered trees flocked with leaves of bright yellows and reds. It offered both surviving wisps of warmth and invigorating embraces of crisp coolness. And best of all, it would occasionally allow little flash-backs to summer, not always Indian Summer days speaking technically, but joyous little summer reruns that warded off a bit longer the encroaching cold shoulder of outright winter.

So the free candy of Halloween was a highly anticipated exclamation point to the month's conclusion, but the best of what October offered had already been given and enjoyed. It had been a month of driving in country lanes and collecting wild bittersweet branches for winter displays inside, a month of vivid colors and bright sunshine illuminating increasingly shorter days. October was summer's last fling. ⌘

# 11 November
## The Family At Table, Including Our Crazy Uncle

Holidays in Iowa, and especially Thanksgiving, meant great family dinners with lots of side dishes; as close to excess as our generally sober and frugal Iowa ways allowed. My father's parents and his sister and her husband lived just across the street from us in Winterset, as I may have told you. That brought our table to eight minimum on any holiday of note, and sometimes to eleven if we were joined by my mother's parents from a county over, and Heinnie a hired man to my paternal grandparents on the farm. Heinnie had moved to Winterset too when they sold their farm and retired, and he became something of a local character as well as a sort of default family member.

They say every family has its crazy uncle. If so, ours was without any competition Uncle Scotty from across the street.

His holiday plates were always heaped impossibly high, largely with mashed potatoes and pools of gravy which threatened to overflow and run onto the table and then the floor. After dinner, as predictably as sunset, he would announce that he felt "a collapsing spell coming on," and head for the sofa to use up far more than his proportional allotment of space.

Scotty was a barber in town (a craft he may have picked up in the military without any formal training I ever knew about) and maintained one of normally two barber shops there. The pleasure for me and my brother in going to his shop was the big assortment of comic books that awaited, but not the haircuts themselves—which we both consistently felt failed to put us in the best frame. For long sections of my school days I just gave up trying to look good and let Uncle Scotty essentially shave my head in what was then called a "Butch" haircut—at least it was neat.

These comic books were never an investment for Uncle Scotty; they were unsold copies left over at the Ben Franklin five and dime store where their top covers had been torn off to earn a refund from the distributer.

## November

My Aunt Ina, who worked at the store, would then bring them home so Scotty could take them to his barber shop to keep his youngest customers quiet while waiting their turn (no one made reservations in those days). This may sound a little wrong, but Ina surely had earned them by virtue of her poor wages after years of working at that store—I think she and the other lady clerks were earning *as much as* seventy-five cents an hour tops by my senior year in high school. When I was offered a summer job that year, I came up with enough manliness to say I couldn't take it for any less than a *whole* dollar an hour, which I got, but for which I was sworn to absolute secrecy.

Scotty and the other barber, who was a member of our church, became the greatest of rivals, at least in Scotty's mind. He was actually probably obsessive about the rival barber, whom we'll call Jerry Smith for purposes of discretion.

Years down the road when Scotty and my aunt visited New York City, my future husband and I took them to dinner in the Yorkville section of Manhattan at a little place we knew was atmospheric, had perfectly adequate food, and was reasonably within our limited budget. This place also offered all-you-can-drink self-serve wine from a tapped barrel for a set price.

As the evening wore on Scotty made a number of trips to the barrel to test out the "all you can drink" aspect. John and I will never be able to forget, and still talk about, the vision of Uncle Scotty sitting in front of another full plate (and glass) with gravy quite literally dripping down his necktie as he announced, "It's a good thing Jerry Smith isn't here; he wouldn't know how to behave in a place like this."

Scotty's love of the grape posed a challenge family-wide. On a driving trip to visit me in New Jersey sometime later, my parents and Scotty's wife conspired to keep things under control by lying to him every time they crossed another state line. Scotty always viewed these line crossings as an opportunity to stop for a bottle or two, but to his frustration he was assured by his companions each time that they were entering another 'dry' state just like the previous one had been.

When they finally got to New Jersey the lie could hold neither water nor wine, so off Scotty went to purchase what he knew this time would be available.

I was then sharing a beautiful old house (mansion, really) with John and another friend. The evening my family arrived, our housemate Robert, who was wonderfully handy in the kitchen, fixed up a meal to his usual high standards, and we all sat around the dining room table in front of the big carved stone fireplace enjoying food and wine in a festive mood.

## Winterset In Time

After a time, we three locals noticed that Scotty's napkin was now on his plate and was disappearing fork-full by fork-full. After an exchanged glance (did *you* see what *I* saw!), Robert at the head of the table calmly asked, "Scotty, would you like another napkin?" Scotty graciously accepted, and proceeded to begin eating it. Luckily we had not yet been able to invest in cloth napkins.

Uncle Scotty, as I mentioned, had acquired a taste for the grape in Europe while serving in the military, where he was an Army MP. He brought this appreciation home when discharged and incorporated it into his small town Iowa life. Whenever I went across the street late in the day, there was Scotty sitting in a broken down easy chair with a big jug of wine next to him on the floor. He would periodically hoist up the jug and take a swig of wine from the bottle.

Even to me as a mere child there appeared to be something incongruous about the scene. Scotty sat there lumped into a big chair wearing only a tee shirt and pants, with grand opera playing on the phonograph, and chugging wine directly from a jug. The scene somehow didn't square with photos I'd seen in magazines of folks drinking wine, or for that matter listening to opera. But while his wine drinking aesthetic was a bit hillbilly, he at least did have opera playing on his phonograph—another cultural plus he had acquired in Europe.

Actually I suppose I shouldn't seem to criticize his imbibing methods since my father had a bit of the same hillbilly drinking style. He, too, bought his wine in huge jugs of questionable quality and kept the current jug 'hidden' on the floor of the closet he used for his work cloths. When he came home at the end of the day he would hoist the jug up to his shoulder and take a big swig—although to his credit that would be the only wine he'd drink that or any evening. I never saw that pattern vary.

To be honest, during school-boy days I always thought Scotty was—well, let's say "queer" for want of a more apt word. Here was a kid who couldn't figure out his own divergent sexuality and mostly at the time thought he was 'straight', but who more-or-less had his uncle pegged as one of *those* people.

I doubt I was the only one in Winterset who thought that, either. The many rustic and earthy types who stepped into Scotty's barber shop fresh from plowing their fields, only to hear opera playing in the background and Scotty discussing Europe with a customer, must have had their questions as well.

For the family the mystery of Uncle Scotty was accentuated by a murky memory of two uniformed military men crossing the snow toward grandpa's farm house, where my aunt was staying while her husband served overseas. What may have been said, what may have been the reason for this official visit, I was never allowed to know. And in general terms it was never spoken of.

Every family has its secrets; I hope I never became one myself despite the prevailing attitudes of the era, and the fact that I, in due course, left the clergy business to the sadness of my parents. I had all of the credentials needed to succeed Scotty as the family black sheep, but if I did come to share his role, no one was unkind enough to point it out to me. Of course, we were Midwesterners, and we seldom spoke of anything more intimate than the current weather. (On the other hand, writing is a form of talking to oneself, so I can't vouch for my own lack of eccentricity even now.)

As a college man I got to visit Europe myself for the first time as part of a group of peers between freshman and sophomore years. At the following Christmas break several of us staged a reunion at the home of one of the girls of this group who lived in Kansas City.

When it was time to go home I caught a ride with some guys, and one of the girls, who had to drive to Wisconsin, and thus to pass through Iowa in any case. Snow started just as we left and before too long we were driving through a classic Midwestern blizzard.

It was obvious we had to stop for the night, and fortunately we did make it as far as Winterset. Our guest bed having been assigned to the girl, my mom quickly arranged with Aunt Ina across the street for the use of her guest room, and I led the two guys over to Grandpa's house.

As we got to the empty guest room on the second floor, a voice came out of the other guest room where Uncle Scotty had installed himself for the night. "What's going on?" "Okay, but open the door and say hello." So I opened the door and my two friends beheld Uncle Scotty buried in blankets, and saying loudly, "You can sleep in here. I'm not homosexual, you know!"

Did the gentleman protest too much? Certainly too much for my comfort in that moment, and especially since I had some misgivings about the veracity of his self-assessment. I've always wondered what thoughts were going through my aunt's head as she heard her husband unnecessarily defending his sexuality at the same time as he was apparently trying to solicit a male sleeping companion for the night.

Scotty led an active social life in Winterset, being a member of veterans' groups, a Mason, and member and occasional deacon of the Lutheran Church. I can't and don't believe he acted out any unapproved urges he may have felt, at least in civilian life. Winterset was not the place one could do such things in any case. Winterset was a place where anyone outside the mainstream buried him/herself in the narrow and the ordinary and knew that was the extent to which they would be permitted any latitude in life.

Uncle Scotty and Aunt Ina were childless. Some people might see that as a clue to his sexuality, but I was never privy to enough adult conversation on such matters to know any of the possible medical ramifications which might have been involved. In fact, I'm not sure if any of the adults did either, or even if my aunt and her husband had ever pursued the matter medically.

They must have wanted children, however, because I can recall an early period of time when adoption was being actively considered. I was very excited to think that I might suddenly have a cousin living right across the street, and how much more interesting family life would be for me when (if) this adoption took place. It never did.

Nevertheless, in his frequently outspoken manner, Scotty did contribute one of the puzzle pieces of sex education I was stringing together while a school-boy. At a family dinner the adults were discussing the impending birth expected by some distant relative couple who had recently married. Scotty contributed to the conversation: "You never know when the first one will arrive," and then repeated this conclusion a few more times, as was his wont.

I was at the stage of knowing about gestation and the normal nine month waiting period involved in such situations. But Scotty had thrown me a bit of a loop here. Did the nine month factor not apply to a first-born child? Did it apply only to the later children of a couple? Was there some medical aspect of a first pregnancy which threw out the usual nine month rule?

I had to go to my mother again to sort this out. She explained that Scotty was merely expounding, loudly, on the fact that the beginning of a pregnancy and the date of a wedding ceremony might not always be coordinated in the expected way. So, nine months was validated as the official medical number, and I was another notch further along in my dance with the birds and the bees.

There was a touch of pathos about Uncle Scotty as well. He decided he wanted to be mayor one time, and spent a lot of hot air talking and planning for that. He did not get to City Hall that way, however. He did arrive finally, but as the part-time janitor in need of extra income beyond his full-time profession. The sad irony of this was not lost on his by-then college aged nephew, and I was sobered that this bigger-than-life man had to have his vulnerable side so publicly exposed in an addicted-to-gossip town.

## THE 'HIRED MAN' MOVES IN

Heinnie was the other (almost) family member who was something of a Winterset character, although he could never have kept up with Uncle Scotty in that department. His real name was Heinrich Schlieline, but I had innocently corrupted that to Heinnie Sunshine as a tiny boy and he henceforth became Heinnie to one and all.

He showed up one fine day at my dad's parents' farm just outside of Greenfield, a little town famous not because I was born there, alas, but because Jesse James decided to stage his first train robbery nearby.

Heinnie had emigrated from Germany, alone, as a late teen or early adult for reasons I never knew (but it was during the 1940s, so one did not have too much trouble guessing) and had essentially apprenticed himself out to Iowa farmers for a living.

He was what Iowans knew as "the hired hand" and had simply taken up residence with my grandparents on that basis. Whenever I stayed with my grandparents as a child, there was Heinnie who lived and ate in the farmhouse, seemingly as much a member of the family as any of us. He had even supplied the name for the farm dog: "Bup," because he had difficulty pronouncing "Pup."

When my grandparents retired and moved to Winterset, it was almost an automatic reflex, I imagine, that Heinnie also moved to Winterset—he wasn't a blood member of our family, but it was really the only family or identity he had at that point, and evidently staying close to us was the only way he could imagine continuing his life. Besides, the farm was gone now and he was beginning to leave behind the days of a young man's strength and vitality.

He drove to town in his incredibly old black two-seater car, which he never considered updating, and bought a little house trailer for which he rented a space in the alley a few steps from our and my grandparents' houses. (Nearly every block in Winterset is bisected by an alley to which every property on the block is exposed in a "back door" sense, a sort of network of circulation vessels which covers garbage collection, delivery of supplies, and anything else a proper citizen would not want to handle through the front door.)

After moving to town, Heinnie earned his keep as an electrician and was much in demand, probably because he was fairly inexpensive. I never had a clue as to how he learned about the domestication of electricity—probably out of a book sometime after moving to America because he had never been formally schooled.

He also took any odd jobs which came his way, including relatively important roles in the seasonal work of blue-grass seed harvesting (which industry probably had its proper name and terminology, although I can't recall them now).

I used to be treated with going along with Heinnie occasionally on one of his grass seed duties, and it was because of this that I was included when his boss and he attended a big farm machinery fair one summer at which the great Adlai Stevenson spoke (former Illinois governor and major intellect who lost the presidency twice to Dwight Eisenhower before service as U.S. Ambassador to the United Nations under John F. Kennedy).

Did that day help head me toward a life-long interest in politics? I was certainly impressed with Stevenson, and thereafter I never thought of myself as a Republican again, although Republicanism remained the political religion of everyone else in my family except eccentric Uncle Scotty.

Sometimes on my outings with Heinnie I had to wait in his little black car while he downed a round or two at his favorite "beer joint," but I never observed him actually drunk and never felt any apprehension about his driving.

He did drink while driving though—apple cider. One time he got ahold of the wrong jug in the store and at the first slug of the stuff, sent the big bottle and contents crashing out of the car window onto the highway. His purchase that day had been labeled "Apple Cider Vinegar" but he had missed one of the three words in his haste.

The theme of daytime 'beer joint' patronage was a bit of a minor theme in the background of small town life, however, usually sufficiently hidden to be nothing more than a little static in the otherwise clear sailing of sunny days. A few years later in early high school I lost a friend because of his father's predilection in that direction.

My friend and I had attended a Bible Camp session in the lakes region of Iowa and returned to Des Moines by Greyhound Bus. His parents and sister had come into the city to drive us back to Winterset. His father, usually a Dr. Jekyll, had even promised all of us we'd go to a movie before the drive home. But first, urgent business called him.

My friend and I were ordered to stand outside the tavern door and not stray. After an hour or so we started to pace a few yards or so back and forth out of sheer boredom. Unfortunately when the father exited his tavern we were at the street corner a few doors away, and Dr. Jekyll turned into a raging Mr. Hyde. The movie was cancelled and the ride home was laden with a little more apprehension than I'd felt riding with Heinnie.

## November

My friend disappeared from my life quickly, I assume out of embarrassment. It was one thing for him to know the world he had inherited as long as he could hide it from outside eyes—it was very much a different thing to be friends with someone who had observed and experienced that world first hand. There was hurt to be felt in Winterset. I was just living in a sweet bubble which managed to avoid most of that hurt.

Heinnie never married, nor to my observation demonstrated any particular interest in women as a younger or middle-aged man. He did, however, acquire a "girlfriend" late in life. Carrie was a widow, on in years herself, and with a bevy of children in her house. Who first took a fancy to whom would be an interesting guess, but soon Heinnie was spending lots of time in her house being mothered with coffee and food.

My parents felt Carrie was trying to take advantage of him—financially at least. When he died of a heart attack, under a house where he had been wiring electricity on his back, she acted the widow. How genuine or intense her emotions may have been—or whether they simply resulted from his having died before they could be legally married—I don't know, of course.

But whatever his romantic status, Heinnie was a constant fixture of my childhood. Nearly always present at family dinners, in his holiday uniform of a clean pair of bib-overalls, he was there seemingly by the same right as any relative. No one ever bothered to look at him as any sort of outsider; he was just a given.

He was simply part of family life. When my brother and I got new bicycles he was right there to help test drive them. "I nemma can crank [peddle], my elebones [knees] keep hitting the steering vheel [handle bar]," he lamented after nearly toppling over in the driveway.

When he died, my dad was named executor and there was a search for any remaining relatives he may still have had in Germany. I don't think any were found, but I recall photos being taken of him in his casket to share if any relatives turned up (which somehow seemed to me a very Winterset, or at least Iowa, thing to be worried about; photos of a dead man, that is).

The funeral package included a limo for relatives to ride following the hearse to the town cemetery, and I found myself perched there with my family and feeling uneasy about it—shouldn't Carrie have been riding in this car? And for that matter, where was Carrie? I don't remember her in any way involved in the funeral—the last time I remember seeing her was at her house the day Heinnie died.

She was in tears that day. I announced to my people that she was acting like the widow and therefore should be treated like the widow. They were skeptical, and I had to admit that they knew more about life in a small town than did I, off as I was at this point exploring wider horizons.

Little boys (some of them could have been Carrie's for all I knew) rode their bicycles along-side and wove inside and outside the funeral procession and I was upset because I thought they were dishonoring Heinnie. My mother suggested that maybe they knew him and were expressing themselves as best they could.

So Heinnie was put to rest in the Winterset cemetery, as would later be Uncle Scotty, and any other characters who may have spiced our little town along the way. It was also the last stop for most of my relatives and most of the adults I remember from childhood, as well as, now, a growing roster of school mates. I've now visited that cemetery many times as a Boy Scout or a high school band member on Memorial Day, dreading the report from the guns of the saluting honor guards, and far too many times as part of a funeral procession for someone I loved. I have no plans to end up there myself, being now a Connecticut Yankee, but that (probably no longer so little) cemetery will remain an unavoidable part of my history in any case. ⌘

# 12 December
## Tinsel That Hangs Straight

December was a hypnotic hybrid of bustling commerce on the town Square and a month-long festive holiday mood. Immediately after Thanksgiving the long strings of colored lights intertwined with real evergreen foliage would be strung from street light to street light around the Square, with each light pole also bearing a wreath of evergreen festooned with a very big red bow.

Colored lights were strung from the very pinnacle of the courthouse tower down to each of the four corners of the Square, proclaiming for miles around that it was now the season of joy and goodwill (and I suppose, proclaiming as well that it was time to come into town and do a little Christmas shopping). Everyone came to the Square to get a first-hand dose of the holiday spirit, and the old timers grumbled that it was too early for all this decorating and why couldn't it wait at least another couple of weeks. Still, no one could deny the sheer magic of the town Square during a light December snowfall.

Folks for the most part did wait a little longer before they started to decorate their yards and the outsides of their houses with strings of lights and replicas of Santa in his sleigh urging on his reindeer. But once they got started, they did not hesitate to try to outdo their neighbors in splendorous displays of brilliant holiday cheer to the point that one almost needed sunglasses to view some of their offerings. Then the December ritual of the evening family drives around town could begin; for the kids and moms a fantasy trip to an imagined Disneyland which blossomed in Winterset once a year like Brigadoon, and for the dads a discreet chance to check out the competition and decide if even more outside lights were going to be needed next year.

Stores on the Square made their contributions to the festivities by putting a little extra effort into their window displays, and by staying open longer than usual at least one or two extra evenings per week in case not everyone had finished their Christmas shopping; an altruistic manifestation of true holiday spirit I have no doubt. There were those who did doubt, however, and a background chorus of the grumblers would get their annual chance to decry the commercialization of Christmas, out of which we were gradually evicting Christ as they were certain to point out.

Our church young folks group would always dutifully try to coax Christ back into Christmas, as you may not be surprised to learn. Mostly this consisted of going caroling, trudging happily through the snow to sing in front of houses occupied by the elderly and infirm, but hoping the cheer being so generously spread would reach even the ears of the healthy and young in neighboring houses.

The highlight of these cheer spreading ventures was reached on the evening we went up the hill to the town hospital and stationed ourselves in a reverberant stairwell to lavish the Christmas spirit on the whole building. Upon occasion characters like Rudolph and elves may have entered into our lyrics, but there was no doubt that the real object of the exercise was to restrain Christ from fleeing Christmas altogether. And nothing even hinting at proselytization was intended. This was small town Iowa so everyone was 'Christian' to begin with, obviously, although some may have been more aware of their status than others. There was simply no one left to convert, just perhaps to encourage to show up in church again at least once during this season of light.

Well, it could not be denied that the holiday joy in the households of the town merchants was enhanced by these weeks of enlivened commercial activity. In the Ben Franklin 'dime store' where I worked weekends and school holidays, boxes were now disappearing from the overhead racks of counters along the walls. These had been accumulating during the year as customers took advantage of the store's "Lay-Away" plan by claiming an object destined to become a Christmas gift and then paying small segments of its price at regular intervals for months on end. Seeing these lay-away boxes disappear inserted a small sadness into the season for me because evidently so many people could not afford to purchase these gifts outright— especially disturbing since nothing in the store cost all that much money to begin with.

Traces of the war still dogged life in Winterset through my childhood years, although since I had not experienced any of the original deprivation myself, I could be blissfully unaware except for wondering about strange rituals like asking truckers to bring back oleo margarine from trips south of the border (Missouri). This turned up in many meals in many guises, but was especially notable in our homemade Christmas cookies.

Don't get me wrong about oleo, Iowans like butter better than margarine but the war (WWII) was still a recent memory and we were still "making do" with lean household budgets. We didn't hold back on the

## December

essentials, like making decorated Christmas cookies, which were ubiquitous in that season, but—they were made with oleo margarine.

Christmas always meant a tree, of course. The lucky among us got to decorate a real tree even though imitation ones, probably heavily flocked with fake snow, were beginning to be popular; probably mostly because one only had to invest in them once.

Out would come the family heirloom ornaments, the strange bubbling lights that usually set fire to at least one house in town per season, and the silvery tinsel.

That damned tinsel—wadded and tangled into clumps because one never bought new but always saved it from past years (for the same reason our cookies tasted like sugared oleo margarine).

I would have been happy to finish decorating the tree by throwing clumps of the stuff on willy-nilly, but Dad resolutely upheld his Germanic heritage by insisting that the thin strips of tinsel hang down militantly straight and one-by-one. So hours were spent untangling wads of little foil strips saved from the previous year and hanging them on the tree so that none touched another. Then I'd stand back to admire our creation, and to admit that, of course, Dad had been right—to *silently* admit this, that is—and to eat yet another margarine cookie.

War generation or not, and maybe precisely because of it, my parents were generous with Christmas presents for their offspring. Under the tree would always be an enormous pile of colorfully wrapped gifts, some with ribbons tied in fancy knots. I knew my mother had been shopping for gifts for months, maybe even all year, and hiding things in various secret spots until time to start decorating and wrapping; and luckily I was never motivated to search out any of the gifts ahead of time, nor did I ever stumble across one by accident.

So the pile got larger under the tree day by day as the alluring holiday approached, just as, when I was four or five, the anticipation and wonder of it all grew day by day. I would stare at the tree my parents had decorated, mesmerized by the glass ornaments which for the most part were refugees from their own childhood Christmases. The fragile glass globes were memorized from concentrated fascination, and every year when they were rediscovered in the back of a closet and redeployed on a new tree, they were friends returning to announce that it was Christmas again—the magic had returned.

Some of our decorations failed to reach the heirloom category but became regulars at the party anyway. My mother always festooned the kitchen windows with some plastic cut-outs of Santa Claus and flying sleds pulled by reindeer, which self-adhered to the glass in a gaudy display which, while cheery, left me a little skeptical of their artistic worthiness. But one could solve that problem, at least temporarily, by adding one's own art to the window, drawing with a finger in the blank sheets offered by the frosty interior panes.

Opening those enticing boxes under the tree was supposed to happen at dawn on Christmas morning; that, at least, was the collective American image. The kids were supposed to race downstairs in their pajamas and start tearing wrapping paper off boxes while Mom and Dad watched, or took home movies. Then Dad would set up the electric train tracks around the tree and Mom would make the hot chocolate. In our house it didn't work quite that way—evidently we were rebels. At least we were church people, and that's ultimately what distorted the iconic pattern.

First there was church on Christmas Eve, an evening service which often featured a children's manger tableau (unless that had taken place the previous Sunday). Then there was another service on Christmas morning. At one of these three, without fail, the young children of the parish were adorned with halos and fake beards and recited short lines they had been ordered to memorize. The hymns were carols everyone knew by heart and the whole scene was as cozy and warm as cuddling by the fireplace. Christmas was for the kids evidently, it had been decided, and it was the job of the adults to slip back into the hopefully happy memories of when they themselves had been kids.

When we got home from church on Christmas Eve the actual kids were tired of the long wait to dive under the tree, and they were ready for a little action. So Mom had devised a solution to keep the boxes intact a few more hours. We were allowed to spill out the contents of the stockings we had left hanging for Santa to fill. This made no sense chronologically because Santa had not yet visited to fill those stockings, but it did successfully postpone the main event until Christmas day. And this was not exactly an empty gesture because our Christmas stockings were not the little anklets we normally wore which would have been able to hold just a few pieces of candy. Instead, by long tradition, we had borrowed stockings for this ritual from our grandmother; long knee stockings she needed to constrain her rebellious leg veins and we boys needed to contain the gifts of a generous Santa who, technically, had not yet actually arrived to distribute them.

Sated by this little preview-of-coming-attractions, everyone was able to get a little sleep before we were packed off to church yet again. Christmas morning service was not very memorable, being as it was perceived mostly as an interruption in the festivities. These festivities resumed at Christmas lunch when Grandpa and Grandma and Aunt Ina and Uncle Scotty came across the snow chocked street, and Heinnie and maybe even our

## December

Greenfield grandparents joined us at table. Scotty was sometimes a little better behaved than his Thanksgiving demonstrations would have predicted, probably because the day's schedule next called for gift opening and no one would tolerate much more of a delay.

Everyone wedged into the living room with the decorated tree and calmly sat in a big circle. This was to be no free-for-all; it was executed instead as a quasi-military drill. One of us boys would be designated the hander-out of gifts and the rounds were alternated between an adult receiving a gift and one of the boys receiving one of his several gifts. As we got older the gift hander-out could simply choose a box and see who the tag said it should be given to, which played havoc with the alternation but seemed to add an element of suspense. After we were finished the room did have the look of the generic Christmas morning festive chaos, so if my brother and I could be distracted from our loot long enough, we were assigned to the clean-up detail. Then a light Christmas dinner of Christmas lunch leftovers, where Scotty was now free to overindulge and then impose one of his trademark "collapsing spells."

If he hadn't already on Christmas Eve, my dad would likely brew up a batch of his famous eggnog for Christmas evening. The adults seemed really fond of this elixir but the kids were allowed to have a cup as well, which obscures whether the recipe called for a touch of whisky—maybe a slight of hand was involved as to when the fun liquid was added. This holiday eggnog was Dad's masterpiece in the kitchen. So far as I can remember the only other time he spent there in a creative mode was when he decided, at any time in the winter, to mix up a big pot of his equally famous oyster soup, most likely a taste and skill he had acquired living on the Gulf in Alabama.

My childhood must have been the heyday of greeting card manufacturers, at least judged by the Christmas season. The unwritten rule seems to have been that one was supposed to send a greeting card to absolutely everyone one knew or had known, whether one saw this person every day or had lost track years ago of everything except their postal address. And every card received demanded a card in return. The process, therefore, extended over a fairly long period. I recall clearly at very least one Christmas day itself when the postman was on duty and made his usual rounds delivering another big haul of colorful, sparkle sprinkled greeting cards. And they kept arriving several days after Christmas as well.

I was too young to worry about theoretical stuff like whether all of this decorating and card sending carried actual religious freight, or whether it was more basically a manifestation of the winter solstice which humans had been observing since long before our particular religion was up and running. I doubt that anyone else in town had such concerns either. It was simply a time when everyone needed the lift in spirits which a celebratory season helped provide. The days were finally starting to get longer again, although it would take a few more weeks to feel much of the impact.

It was not until decades later that I realized what was missing from these family scenes—the rest of our family which was marooned outside in the cold: our pets. This revelation came because God had favored my adult family life with the most wonderful stray dog anyone could have loved. He lived inside and built up his Christmas anticipation as our ersatz child. And he learned on his own how to unwrap Christmas boxes from under the tree very delicately, removing the paper without a hint of damage to the container or to the gift itself (many of which had his name on their tags). I could see then that Christmas was, indeed, for the kids. But I could also see that my childhood Christmases had frozen out certain key members of the family.

Pet dogs during my childhood were strictly outside creatures. We lived in town, but our culture was rural and most adults had learned their ways on the farm or from a worldview permeated with farm ways and habits. Dogs were loved but they were animals, and on the farm animals lived outside the house. So dogs usually had a shelter, just as the other animals had their barns and coops.

A dog's home was a dog house, and for heat a bed of hay was spread on its floor to warm the sleeping animal as the hay slowly decayed. None of my boyhood dogs lived with us inside the house, until the very last one who moved inside after I had left for college. This little dog had managed to blind himself by chasing power lawn mowers incessantly until years of debris hitting his eyes had rendered him totally blind. My mother took him in as an act of kindness, and attended him as carefully as later she would attend to her own invalid mother. When the time came, she buried him in a hand shoveled grave by the railroad tracks which ran aside our home, just as all of our family pets had been laid to rest, and just like it was done on the farm. ⌘

# 13 Sunday
## The Lord Shares His Day With the Open Road

Sunday mornings were not for sleeping in as folklore might have suggested—Iowans are too industrious for sleeping late in any case. The first problem of the day for me was my newspaper delivery route, which meant getting up before any evidence of light outside and going to the distribution point just off the town Square to claim my allotted supply of big, fat Sunday editions of *The Des Moines Register*, 'the newspaper Iowa depends on' (at some point along the way it appears the language police did force a correction).

This involved pulling a sled to the site and loading it up in the winter, or riding my bike there in the summer and leaving with a heavy yellow shoulder bag of newspapers. Occasionally, if I was not feeling well, or if the weather was severe, my mother would drive me from block-to-block and wait while I delivered papers to both sides of the street on foot, before moving the car on to the next block. Mostly, however, it was a one-boy endeavor plying familiar streets full of dogs which gradually came to tolerate and ignore me as I plodded up to each front porch to leave the newspaper conveniently, and dryly, behind the screen, or storm door.

Then, workday finished, I could count on a hearty Iowa breakfast at home to compliment reading the Sunday newspaper comics, beckoning in their resplendent colors. My parents were both raised on farms, and were deeply indoctrinated into the Iowa religion of a breakfast fit to sustain Paul Bunyan for a long day of tree-felling.

We knew about breakfast cereal that came in cardboard boxes, of course, and sometimes on regular weekdays might even have sunk so low as to make do with just a bowl of it for a quick breakfast. But not on Sundays. Sundays were a day of rest, which meant someone, usually Mom, had to go to a great deal of work to produce a hot home-cooked feast involving, at minimum, eggs, meat, maybe oatmeal or cornbread, and pancakes or waffles (under pressured circumstances perhaps mere toast would have sufficed for the pancakes; speaking of which, did you know sliced bread was invented in Iowa? Another of our food related contributions to mankind).

Then it was time for the need-it-or-not hot shower and dressing for church. And people *did* dress for church. As a junior male, it was my duty to wear a necktie to church and a little later a jacket, if not a full suit. I can't remember ever going to church with an open collar, although I presume I was not wearing a necktie as a baby when I was baptized.

We'd then pile into the family car for the first time that day and Dad would steer in his rather uncommitted way (taking corners with just one hand on the steering wheel which uses up a lot of road space). While I never heard him complain or rebel, I suspect he was protesting in his mild way. Although it was his German Lutheran heritage which bound us to church, it was my convert mother who was the enforcer.

I have no doubt my dad would have been fairly happy to spend Sunday mornings in a variety of other ways. Once in a while, especially during the summer, the menfolk were grudgingly granted a day off for fishing or whatever non-churchly attraction beckoned. But mostly it was duty before pleasure, and even I, a rather committed church mouse, understood that church was indeed a duty rather than a pleasure.

Sunday church consisted of two parts, "Sunday School" and "the Service." The school portion was mostly for the children and mostly for them to learn the characters and stories of the Old Testament—essential information which surely would come in handy later as they lived their successful adult lives.

The service itself was for everyone (the kids just released from Sunday School did not get a reprieve from hour number two). Parents who had dropped off their kids for Sunday School began to return for the main event.

One thing which can be said to the credit of our congregation is that the service always started on time. This was not so much a credit to our sense of punctuality, however, but arose more from a deeply inbred modesty. No one wanted to sit in the front few pews, so there was a weekly race for the coveted pews in the back of the church. Latecomers were penalized by having to sit closer to the chancel. Actually, maybe the operative emotion wasn't modesty, come to think about it. Maybe we just didn't want the preacher to catch us nodding off during the long sermon, which nearly always was a lecture on some aspect of St. Paul's mysterious way of thinking.

The first event on the program was to sit through an organ prelude. Our church organists were always pianists who were drafted into service because

## Sunday

they could plow their way through a hymn with some degree of credibility. Our church organ was a home reed instrument which had been electrified with a vacuum cleaner motor to eliminate the need to pump air with foot pedals, which it did—although the motor did make its own contribution to the resulting sound. I suspect these organ preludes were often some sort of improvisation on the hymns for the day which the organist had been practicing through the week.

We were Lutherans, which meant following a set "liturgical" service composed of prescribed declarations and prayers which followed the same patterns and used the same words Sunday after Sunday. The only variations were the sermons, the particular hymns selected for the day, and the color of the paraments hanging from the altar and lecterns, which varied with the liturgical season. The pastor always vested for services, although in the sober German Lutheran tradition we'd inherited that meant only a black academic gown for any Sunday of the year, including our "high holy days" such as Easter and Christmas. In due course our pastors added a long fat ribbon of material draped around their necks and called a "stole," which carried the same color as the paraments of the particular liturgical season. This, in a town with a largely Protestant population, was about as 'high church' as things got if one ignored whatever the Catholics were up to, and considering that the few Episcopalians around town never managed to keep their own place going very long at a time and mostly had to settle-in with the Lutherans.

These services were not only somewhat rigid, they were in truth also somewhat dull despite the bits of music dribbled in along the way. The sermons were long lectures usually focusing on what St. Paul wrote, or really meant to write, or should have written, or the pastor wished he had written. The hymns were timidly sung denials of the great Lutheran choral tradition which we continued to claim anyway. But we at least had done our Sunday duty; we had gone to church. Life now could forge guiltlessly into another week.

After church sometimes my dad would stop on the Square for a little indulgence from The Candy Kitchen, usually a bag of caramel corn: a concoction of popcorn clumped together with a thick dried but still sticky syrup and heavy with added peanuts. Then it was off to Benoit's to shop for lunch, which often enough was sliced liverwurst in hamburger rolls.

Winterset had a handful of neighborhood grocery stores in addition to two or three (depending on the year) larger 'supermarkets' which were normally closed on Sundays—quite a profusion for a town of never quite 4,000 population. Some were tiny affairs good mostly for kids stopping in for a treat while walking home from school. Two of them, Allguyer's and

Benoit's, sort of hovered between the supermarket and the hole-in-the-wall category. Benoit's was for Sundays. Allguyer's was for when Mom forgot something while grocery shopping and sent the kids over on their bikes to pick it up. Mrs. Mack's, a little grocery store around the corner from us, was for desperation.

One was never sure if being a customer of Mrs. Mack was a help to her or a curse upon her. Her store was the bottom floor of her frame house, tucked into a little corner cut out from the North Ward Elementary School yard. When one opened the front door, Mrs. Mack could be seen down the hall in her enormous overstuffed chair watching her small black & white television. She then had to struggle to her feet and wield her cane to hobble into one of the front two rooms which comprised the mini-grocery store. For adults Mrs. Mack was a last resort. For kids, however, her tiny emporium was an ever-ready source of sweets, although the candy bars were sometimes wormy from sitting near a sunny window and the ice cream was usually foamy from having been thawed and refrozen. Nevertheless, a constant supply of our nickels and dimes did find their way into Mrs. Mack's coffers.

This rather remarkable array of food shops had the town covered in all its neighborhoods except one. The far west end, a little tonier and a little more pretentious than the rest of town, did have one gas station on its outer extreme which carried some deli items. But it lacked a solid neighborhood grocery—except in my dreams. For some reason I was convinced that there had to be such a little store there. I'd seen it so often in my dreams. It was more varied in what it offered than any of the others, and it had an unusual and somewhat more daring architecture than the others. It was full of great open tables of fresh vegetables, and its selection of candies and cookies was more exotic than any of the others could offer. I looked for it sometimes when riding my bicycle around town, and when I came home to visit as an adult I was always a little suspicious that I might discover it as I drove around the familiar streets of the west end. I never saw it when I was awake, however.

Sunday lunch always had an impromptu aura which lent a certain festivity. The weekday rules of solid meat and potatoes sobriety, at lunch as well as dinner, were suspended in favor of something easy to throw together, which lent a happy casualness. Unless a major holiday fell on Sunday, the day was unofficially a mini-break for Mom from "slaving over a hot stove," at least after breakfast.

Sunday afternoons were for family drives unless the winter roads were too risky from ice or the summer roads were too stifling—air conditioning in cars in those days being merely a lowered window or two. We'd pile into

## Sunday

our car for a great adventure, although we'd experienced it many times before and nothing this time was scheduled to be different in the slightest. We never stopped for a meal or for any reason other than the occasional need to refuel. A Sunday drive was exactly what it promised to be and nothing more: a drive; yet it was the highlight family activity of the week measured from any angle.

The men always sat in the front seat, with the back seat reserved for the women and youngest children. Being the first-born I got to sit with the men, while my brother, although only four years younger, was restricted to riding with the women. So I was wedged between my father, who always did the driving, and my Uncle Scotty who amply occupied the front passenger seat.

Sundays in the car I became aware of my father as an individual. His distinctive masculine odor had a faint attraction which sometimes surprised me, and which I never would have expected I could still recall clearly when I became the age he was then—a mixture of his Sunday shaving lotion, his occasional cigars, and, I guess, just him. That strange pleasure never lasted long on a Sunday drive, however, because Uncle Scotty would soon light up one of his ubiquitous cigarettes. This would generate a big cloud inside the car and lowered all of our life expectancies long before the medical establishment figured out that cigarette smoke, whether first hand or second hand, might not be the greatest benefit to one's health.

Iowa was prairie land and generally flat except for very gently rolling hills. For some wonderful geological reason parts of Madison County, however, had been granted the dramatic pleasures of steep limestone outcroppings, tall hills, and deep river valleys. So we would leave Winterset, set on its own rather high plateau, and drive west into a valley which was hugged on either side by heavily wooded hills. The hills, the river, everything had long ago been memorized in detail, yet the drama was always fresh somehow, perhaps because driving in any other direction from town would have yielded mostly flatness. Then the road gradually settled into farm country again and the hills would be replaced by another supreme beauty, the deep black plowed earth of the plains.

We'd continue west, aiming for Lorimor, a town which didn't really exist beyond being a name on the official state road map. After Lorimor the next town was Podunk, which didn't exist beyond a rumor. Eventually we'd arrive at actual towns, and the highways in those days always took us directly into the center where often a county courthouse was anchoring the scene (offering a satisfying comparison to the magnificent Madison County courthouse at Winterset's center, and leaving us a bit smug at the architectural advantage we'd soon return to at home). Nonetheless these prairie towns could be charming, each with its own distinctive character, which was almost a miracle in and of itself. (After my time there Iowa started to urbanize, evidently, because the 2010 census managed to find 360 people in Lorimor and 30 in Podunk. My educated guess is that the density, however, is still not terribly high in either place.)

Big cities were avoided by tacit agreement of the adults, although that was an easy rule to follow in rural Iowa where "big" and "city" seldom appeared in the same sentence anyway. We did, once, drive as far as Joplin, Missouri, on a Sunday afternoon, but otherwise I was usually left without the urban fix I was gradually beginning to crave. Mostly, however, the pleasures of a Sunday afternoon drive were tied to the black gold of Iowa's incredibly rich soil and the delights it offered in seemingly endless oceans of corn fields. And such drives could always yield a jackpot of Iowa richness in their destinations—fields of shockingly colorful tulips in Pella, or endless fields of flowers awaiting harvest as garden seeds in Shenandoah.

Later, by the time I was in high school, the utter charm and simplicity of these Sunday drives was beginning to erode without our understanding that we were losing a way of life. The Eisenhower Interstate Highway system was beginning to be built, encircling Des Moines and dividing the state into roughly even quarters. Soon driving was to leave behind any semblance of being a celebration of life or discovery and become merely a utilitarian means of getting from one place to another in the least possible amount of time. And to just as sad effect, the state was beginning to remove any charm from its highway system, gradually making the concrete ribbons run as straight as arrows, and creating by-pass roads around even such metropolises as Winterset. No longer would the main highways take traffic into the centers of Iowa towns.

Seeing the super highways being built, divided into more than the standard Iowa two lanes, was nonetheless an excitement which seemed to suggest we were on the verge of modernity and maybe even urbanity. As each segment of the Interstate system around Des Moines was finished in turn, people would flock to drive on it and experience for themselves the thrill of multiple lanes. Questions of gravity such as whether one was supposed to drive on the inside lane to leave traffic uninhibited to enter and exit from the outside lane, or whether one was supposed to keep to the right except to pass as on the old highways—such questions became heated debates over coffee as the more placid ways of life receded from us.

By the time I was a student at the University of Iowa this growing network of super highways actually offered a little last taste of the pleasures of childhood. Few of us, as students, had a car to use in testing the new highways out; we still got to and from campus by such retro means as rail.

## Sunday

So my housemates and I figured out we could rent bicycles and use the unfinished Interstate highways as an unrestricted and deliciously smooth cycling network. Once a housemate and I rented bikes and made the whole distance between Iowa City and the Hoover Presidential Library in West Branch on freshly dried smooth concrete without a single other vehicle to distract from the pleasure.

Town folks were still besotted with their cars, and increasingly so as the family car gradually reproduced into the family fleet. Then news came that Winterset would have its chance to become a 'real' city—the state highway commission was planning to run tests to find out if we deserved our own traffic signals at the two busiest corners of the courthouse Square. Black rubber pressure hoses were fixed into place from corner to corner in four directions at each intersection, ready to count the number of vehicles which crossed on a daily basis.

Winterset went into high alert. Civic pride was now at stake. Everyone in town suddenly inherited the civic duty of driving over the black tubes as often as possible every day. The traffic count had to be forced as high as possible no matter how inconvenient it was for the local drivers. My elders would get into their cars for no other reason than to go to the town Square and drive around the block over and over until exhaustion suggested the mandate could wait to begin again tomorrow. This period probably produced the only actual traffic jams the town would ever experience. We did get our stop lights. Then the traffic around the Square leveled off again to its normal languid levels.

By dusk Sunday the driving was over and the car back in its garage. Supper, never "dinner" except when I referred to it, was a casual follow-up to lunch, and probably just another round of whatever we'd eaten at lunch. If I'd been conscientious on Friday or Saturday I was then free to watch television. If I'd been self-indulgent I had to scramble to finish homework. All in all probably not much different of a Sunday from that of most of my town classmates in that post-war quasi-somber period of the mid-twentieth century. The farm kids had a different weekend, however. They had their ever-dependent animals to attend. ⌘

# 14 Monday
## Wild Flowers for a Tame Boy

Monday meant off to school again, a place that was part sanctuary and part punishment for most boys. At least for me for the first seven years it was an extremely short commute of just across one street to the next block. I'd leave our house on the corner, cross the railroad tracks, cross the street, then walk up past Mrs. Mack's mini-grocery to the school which consumed the balance of Mrs. Mack's block.

The school house was as stereotypical as the cleverest architect could have hoped to create, sitting in its red brick bulkiness and hoisting a great bell tower into the sky—a bell tower which alerted the whole neighborhood not only to the beginning and end of the school day, but to the beginning and end of morning and afternoon recess periods and the start and finish of lunch hour. This being the middle of the twentieth century and the middle of Iowa, only the farm kids who had been bussed into town ate lunch on the playground out of paper bags; the town kids trudged off to their mothers' kitchens for hot food and a quick turn-around.

The school was so close to my house that for several grades I had classes in rooms which looked down and over for an unrestricted view of the whole family property. I can remember the calls of classmates to rush to the window in third grade to see fire engines spraying down my parents' smoking garden behind the house. They had asked the town to dump leaves gathered in the autumn into our large vegetable garden to build up the soil, and evidently we'd accidently collected a glowing cigarette butt as well along the way. Eventually I was entrusted with a little corner of that garden to tend myself, and my very first crop was from a package of zinnia seeds. That tiny entry into the ranks of gardeners, however, propelled me into a life of botanical fixation which has lasted well beyond childhood.

Or, did my botanical fascination actually begin much earlier? My first memory is of red berries which grew on a vine encircling a concrete birdbath column. I was perhaps as old as three, or maybe not even that old.

After we moved to Winterset when I was four, into one of the two houses by the railroad tracks which would be our family compound for all of my years as a school boy, there were more plants claiming their places in my emerging memory. I'd walk on the tracks, with my mother on guard and carrying my baby brother, and we'd go perhaps two blocks down line which seemed almost the equivalent of a foreign adventure. And I was besotted by the weeds growing along the tracks, mostly nettles which flourished outside the narrow gravel shoulders that the train workers sprayed with creosote. The most engrossing and joyous discoveries were the occasional thistles which had escaped their intended doom and were blooming in the brightest, deepest purple I had yet seen, their flowers little bunches of upright clumps poking upward as high as my knees.

As we grew older these adventures could take us into hidden country lanes where the alluring orange and red of bittersweet twisted around trees in a show of lavish generosity. Mom would let us break off little pieces of the woody stems to take home for bouquets which would last until they were too dusty to escape housekeeping. But she always warned us not to take too much, counselling as she did about every flower we wanted to pick that it would not grow back again. Of course, the bittersweet was actually an invasive species; another of the weeds which I loved so much as a boy (my dad called such things "volunteer" flowers).

By the time I was old enough to go into the lawn mowing business, I'd moved from weeds to cultivation and began to avidly collect Irises. The process involved begging a few rhizomes from each of my lawn customers, all of whom it seemed had plenty of these gorgeous clumps of tall flowers growing somewhere in their yards. Eventually I accumulated quite an extensive collection, with Irises of seemingly every imaginable color fighting for whatever yard space my parents would allow me to take over.

All of these plants were nearly as much childhood friends as were the kids I played and worked with. Beside our garage, in a tiny strip of land next to the gravel alley, a wonderful stand of hollyhocks would appear each year like magic, taller than me, and bearing a wild assortment of colors in their flowers. I looked forward to seeing them every summer almost as much as the joyous return of school friends in the autumn. It would take me until university botany class, however, to realize I was reuniting with these friends only in alternate generations—I actually had two sets of hollyhock friends, one set of which was always hiding from me waiting to replace the other in their sneaky biennial conspiratorial way.

Even at play the botanical bug seems to have had a big hold on me. My friends and I loved to go hiking in a wooded, somewhat hilly area at the edge of town known as "Kippy's Hollow." As usual, I found myself intrigued by the plant life, and would often pull up an evergreen tree seedling and stuff it in my jeans pocket for the walk home. Then I'd negotiate for a place I could replant it—surprisingly several of these took and had become large trees by the time I moved on to college. One of my little seedlings, this one a conifer I found at a nursery, stands beside that house to this day, now towering over it and having spread almost to its width.

It's hard to say whether the biggest botanical thrill was in planting and moving around specimens, or in the accidental discoveries of wild plants of often incredible beauty such as the honeysuckle or the red and purple wild columbines which could turn up in the most unexpected places. Winterset seemed to have no end of little treasures to be discovered and cherished, like the white violets which sometimes hid among the oceans of their blue kinfolk.

## ANOTHER SIDE TO THE COIN

Clearly I'd inherited something basic about being an Iowan in my love of vegetation and cultivation. But there was something else basic about me of which I had no idea of the origins. My people were rural folks, albeit now transplanted to small town life. The closest either of my parents had of an urban experience was when my father grew up just outside Mobile, Alabama, but even that was on a farm. For some reason I possessed a nascent urban streak, untraceable genetically or even culturally as far as I could discern.

Growing up, Des Moines was Mecca for me. She always beckoned seductively from her safe distance of thirty or so miles, promising glories at which Winterset could only hint.

Whenever either of my parents had to drive into the city I was eager to tag along if it wasn't a school day. These were usually quick in-and-out business trips, to the Des Moines Iron company or another supplier of Dad's machine and welding shop, and the trip almost never allowed for another stop. They also followed the same route I'd seen over and over, but just to be able to look out of a car window and observe a city-scape, albeit it of a fairly tame magnitude in those days, galvanized my imagination and fed my soul in a mysteriously satisfying way. Each trip, no matter how short and routine, reassured me that the city was still there and that Winterset, loveable as she was, did not represent the outside limit of urban possibilities.

It's probably fair to say (admit?) that Des Moines back then was only a rural person's idea of a big city. As I may have mentioned, some people took mischievous delight in calling her just an overgrown country town. But, she was **MY** big city and I took supreme delight in savoring her riches whenever circumstances gave me any kind of opening. I loved the little

## Monday

knots of businesses which appeared in the middle of residential neighborhoods, like mini-towns plopped down here and there as if by accident. I was always thrilled to admire the Equitable Insurance building downtown, a full and glorious eighteen stories high (Iowa's lone 'skyscraper' then, but well under half the height of today's tallest Des Moines building) and to stand on the streets of that central intersection which was actually nearly fully shaded by tall buildings on every corner. I loved watching the buses the locals called "curbliners," powered by arms which brushed a network of overhead electrical wires for power as they rode over downtown pavement which had covered over the trolley rails of their predecessors.

Des Moines even had a tiny (at that time) art museum—talk about big city sophistication!—which we drove past on one of our routine ways out of town. Later on that exit route we passed a large stone church-appearing structure with stained glass windows which was actually a synagogue, another hint of the rich variety of city life—in Winterset we had no religious group more exotic than the Baptists. The other routine route went past the airport from which one could fly non-stop to fabled places like Chicago and Denver, another clue that the world knew we were there and was not entirely ignoring us. The airport even had a well-regarded restaurant from which the planes could be seen landing and taking off. People, it was humored, used this restaurant as a weekend and holiday destination, but I was left only guessing what the experience might be like owing again to my family's frugality (or relative poverty; children could not always calculate the fine points of such questions).

What Des Moines did not seem to have in general back then were good restaurants, or at least not many and not very fancy ones. Of course, as I just admitted I was at a disadvantage in calculating both the quantity and the level of quality because my parents out of both inclination and financial sobriety would not have patronized them in any case. I knew of only one "fancy" restaurant downtown—Babe's, an Italian legend onto itself during my school days. My parents would never have considered eating there, being frugal, down-to-earth, and probably culturally intimidated as well. By the time I was an adult visitor to Des Moines from the wicked East, I took my widowed aunt for a lunch at Babe's, only to discover that by then it was just a glorified pizza parlor, and soon to evaporate from the downtown Des Moines scene altogether, yielding to numerous new very good restaurants any town in the country would be proud to claim.

When my parents, usually with Aunt Ina and Uncle Scotty along, decided we could eat in a 'fancy' downtown Des Moines restaurant it was Bishop's Cafeteria. This was, I think, part of a chain and hardly something

## Winterset In Time

to write home about, but still a dazzling experience if one had driven into town from almost anywhere else in Iowa at the time. My own indelible memory of the place is a big slice of layer cake which means perhaps that the food was fairly routine and lacking in gourmet subtlety. Still, I grew up sure in my conviction that eating at Bishop's was a true city experience and that folks in, say, New York, had no real advantage on us as we pushed our trays along the track and chose the dishes which appeared most appetizing.

Our big leap in restaurant quality came during my high school years when a Howard Johnson chain restaurant opened on Grand Avenue and we could order those very appealing fried clams along with much of the rest of the country, including the sophisticated East.

After finishing our gourmet lunch at the cafeteria we'd usually walk around downtown a bit, and if so, would almost certainly stop at the Katz Drug Store, open on Sundays and thus about the only downtown store we could enter. I'm sure this store was a real pharmacy where people filled prescriptions, but that aspect was totally lost on me as a school boy. I loved Katz because they sold the important stuff in life, mostly toys and lots of them—aisle after aisle of fascinating merchandise not found on shelves in Winterset. We seldom made an actual purchase, but liked simply being in Des Moines itself, just looking was reassuring that Winterset did not represent the sum-total of life's options. A few years later the Katz chain took over a failed grocery supermarket near downtown and opened a gigantic version of itself—a true wonderland offering anything and everything I could imagine that anyone would want to purchase. There, with a few dollars of lawn mowing money in my pocket, I bought my first record player and a couple 45 rpm discs which I then played at home until the grooves expired into a scratchy silence.

Des Moines, despite the cynicism of the "overgrown country village" naysayers, had some superlatives going for it, as well as a handful of near-miss almost superlatives. For one, it had what everyone seemed to agree was "the world's largest legitimate theater" downtown, in addition to its grand ornate movie palaces. It was there, swallowed up in a sea of balcony seats, that I heard my first *Messiah* and my first Broadway musical, both followed up later with many more at Lincoln Center and on Broadway itself. It was there we went for Boy Scout Jamborees and political rallies. The other obvious superlative was the grand Iowa State Fair, which we understood to be the country's largest (some Texans evidently begged to differ with our assessment) and, in any case certainly the country's finest. No Iowan ever doubted that!

And Des Moines was in competition for a couple of other titles which, to face reality, probably only landed us in second place. We were 'Insurance

## Monday

City' if one didn't count Hartford, and in fact there was a long period of non-stop air service between Hartford and Des Moines for that reason, extending periodically until the 2020 pandemic which scrambled the whole country's air route system. And we were "Rubber City" if one didn't count Akron. We were farm equipment city if Peoria was taken out of contention.

And to my mind Des Moines was one of the most beautiful river cities one could imagine—at least until one encountered Paris much later in life. Nothing I could imagine could be as urban-beautiful as the series of symmetrically placed gracefully arched carved stone bridges over the Des Moines River, connecting the two sides of downtown.

The allure of Des Moines during my school days probably said more about me somehow than about either Des Moines or Winterset. Winterset was actually self-sufficient and one could have stayed entirely within her borders without being deprived of any necessity. The first time I bought an article of clothing in Des Moines was as an adult, and for a time Winterset even had a better restaurant than the ones my family patronized in Des Moines. The irony of the times was that as Winterset gained population later in the twentieth century it started losing self-sufficiency and began depending increasingly on Des Moines for life's basics rather than just its frills.

Later in life I'd live for a time in New York City itself. That was great, but New York never replaced Des Moines in my heart, nor ever seemed more urban or more sophisticated than Iowa's big town. I was simply a doggedly loyal Iowan no matter where circumstance placed me. Even now when I can get back to Iowa there is an urban thrill to visiting Des Moines that escapes me in far larger places. John and I have lived for decades now in a city with a metropolitan statistical area population of over one-third of Iowa's entire statewide population, but any thrill from being 'downtown' still belongs to Des Moines. ⌘

# 15 Tuesday
## More Words

'Once upon a time' small children would sprawl on the floor of a downstairs room in the Winterset public library to hear the ritual fairy tales of childhood revealed to them by volunteer readers. As they grew a bit, some of them discovered that the library had even more than Uncle Remus to offer. My own later explorations yielded an entire wall of books about the history of Iowa, and I became a school-boy addict of information about the governors whose names peppered our map as town names and of other places I stored up in my mind as someday imperative to see for myself.

Even one of my pet dogs spent time at the library, although his time was outside in the fresh air waiting for me to emerge again so we could go home, me on my bike and he faithfully running along beside it. After one library visit I came outside and he wasn't on the steps waiting so I pedaled home without him. When he didn't show up there for a couple of hours, I started to worry and went back to the library. There he was sitting on the steps still waiting for me to emerge; evidently having mistimed a rest break and missed my original departure.

In school before we'd learned to read sufficiently for the town library to wield its magnetism, our teachers continued to read the classic literature of American childhood to us as a dessert course after a hard day's labor in the vineyards of nouns and verbs and the construction of simple sentences. So after "See Jane run" and "Sit, Spot, good dog" we would take a breather toward the end of the school day in second grade while our teacher, Miss Blee, read a more complicated story than "Dick and Jane" to us.

One of these excursions into more advanced literature evidently got the best of one of our classmates one day, and he fell into a deep sleep at his desk. Miss Blee saw this situation as an opportunity for either a tremendously humorous prank or a fiendishly clever object lesson of some sort, or maybe both.

She pulled over a chair and stood on it to reach up to the big clock hanging over the classroom door, and moved the hands from three PM to five PM. Then she instructed us to leave the room as quietly as possible, barely able to contain her own amusement. The script called for poor Gene to wake up, see the clock and panic, then run out of the now almost empty school building fearing that he'd miss dinner. The actual outcome of the plot may have been lost to history, at least I can't remember that we were ever given an update. Gene did show up for class the next day, however, looking no worse for his adventure.

Anyway many of us (at least me, in any case) did go on to rely on the town library for book reports, research, and satisfaction of general curiosity about the little areas of life we encountered along the way. Somehow I'm grateful that I was a pre-internet child. Researching with books was a little slower, but their tangibility was a satisfying joy in and of itself.

Our library was a very handsome stone and brick building just a block off the Square, set back from the street on both sides of its corner perch, and providing another little vest pocket park which gave the town its mildly continental charm. It was a gift of Andrew Carnegie and his foundation, which had provided so many libraries to American towns in its day. Later the town would move its library to a defunct auto dealership a block off the other side of the Square and convert the Carnegie building into town hall. The library got a good deal more space and the town got a very handsome headquarters, but the whole transfer never seemed quite proper to me, nor sufficiently grateful to Mr. Carnegie's largess.

## ADDITIONAL SEX ED, WINTERSET STYLE

Seventh grade, more grandly known in Winterset as Junior High School, brought major changes to the classroom routine we'd known as younger kids. Instead of one teacher in one room for the whole day, suddenly we rotated among several teachers and several rooms for classes in specific subjects—math, art, history and so forth. But we could not yet choose which subjects we wanted to study; some freedom in that direction had to wait for high school. In junior high the class decisions were made for us, and one of the oddest, in my view, was that we had what could be fairly be termed a course in social nudity. Swimming along in the peaceful waters of grade school we had no idea that the Winterset public school system had secret plans to turn us into communal nudists.

One of the discoveries awaiting us when we left our North Ward years was that recess morphed from a do-it-yourself project into enforced organized athleticism. For a guy like me who preferred the library to the ball field this called for some ingenuity, although mine never advanced much beyond staying as far in the backfield as possible and praying that balls would be hit only in the other direction. When it was time to return to classes, however, a strange new ritual was inserted which didn't allow any escape routes.

Before we were allowed to return to our studies we had to take off every stitch of clothing and spend several minutes crammed together in a fairly small room. No explanation was given for this new requirement, so for those of us who had managed to expend very little physical effort on the ball field it seemed pointless—pointless but a bit unnerving. Communal nudity had to be a completely new concept to most of us, let alone a completely new experience, and even the very concept felt vaguely threatening to a nice church boy like me.

Evidently the school board was not satisfied that we had done our nudist duty adequately as seventh and eighth graders, so they extended the communal showers into high school—four more years of nakedness among peers at least twice a week. But the gang showers were beginning to feel even more awkward than they had in junior high. Our bodies had been busy developing further in the interim, and some of us, at least, had gone from being gangly, scrawny little guys into something a little more noteworthy. And for some of us (I presume; at least for me) this fact was a further complication.

It's unclear to me how we were supposed to utilize the training in nudity we were being given by the school system. The people who ran things must have thought it through and decided that we would benefit in some way from this aspect of our continuing education. Still, it was not easy to imagine the practical aspects of our developing skill in standing around in groups without any clothes on. There were no nudist colonies in Iowa in need of a pipeline of potential new members or executive talent, at least none that I knew of. And to the best of my knowledge no one from Winterset ever went on to become a star in the pornography business either.

But then what's a little nudity among friends you might be thinking. Evidently for most guys it was just another way to bond; an excuse to snap towels at each other and fool around in various other ways which evidently demonstrated comradery. And by high school most guys were into team sports for a season, or even every sporting season, so gang showers and communal nakedness had become (I'm guessing) entirely routine for them.

But some of us (I'm guessing again; statistically I couldn't have been the only one) were enjoying these little nude-fests less and less as time went on. We were the ones for whom nature had different plans, and for us the gang showers became torture; just the opposite of exercises in bonding. For us these little festivals of communal nudity on school time became exercises in keeping one's eyes open but not seeing anything.

## Tuesday

So, just to name one graphic example, I never saw an adolescent boy in the gang showers experiencing a physical manifestation of hormonal excitement—but then I didn't allow myself to look anyway, so who knows what might actually have been going on.

The boys who were afflicted with an inadequate appreciation of the physical attributes of their female classmates, you probably are thinking, should have been in mini-heaven showering with their male classmates. Life doesn't (or at least didn't back in those days) work that way for teen boys struggling with their sexuality, unfortunately. Not, at least, for boys who didn't yet have a name for guys like themselves, and were trapped in the middle of the twentieth century in a small Iowa town where no one was going to tell them that name either—probably because no one thought that the boys of our healthy little town could possibly need to know it.

If I had played my cards right, graduating from Winterset High School and going off to college should have brought an end to this torturous enforced nudity. But I wanted to become a clergyman and assumed without much research that I should enroll at Wartburg College in northern Iowa because each of our church's pastors during my childhood had graduated from that school. So off I went to Wartburg, only to discover that I'd been betrayed twice over—not only did the school have mandatory PE classes with the resulting mandatory gang showers in the gym, but also that the only way to shower in my residential dorm was in a big open room which, at any time of day one could choose, had at least a few fully naked young men on display.

Well, this was college and I was growing up. I still hated the PE classes, but the showers were becoming less onerous. In fact, these college gang shower experiences might have even been becoming, if not exactly interesting, at least finally rather routine—routine, but not joyous. I still could not allow myself to look, or at least to look carefully enough to risk being obvious about it—and beside that, I still didn't fully understand even that I might *want* to look, and definitely not *why* I might want to look.

Anyway, when I transferred to the University of Iowa half way through my college career I was apprehensive enough to do some advance research. I would live in a house with just a one-guy-at-a-time shower and there were no required PE classes. I certainly was not going to get into organized sports, so gang nudity was finally lifted off my plate of private misery.

All of this is not to suggest, however, that the Winterset public schools were not trying to be seriously helpful in occupational preparations. They were, I think, but I believe they missed the boat by taking too simple a view of boys will be boys, and girls will be girls.

Society in those Ozzie and Harriet days had basically decided that the vast majority (actually, the assumption was most likely ALL) of the girls were going to be mothers and homemakers, and that the vast majority (if not all) of the boys were going to be fathers with a household to maintain and support. Any stragglers who might not fit neatly into these cozy Norman Rockwell images had to be allowed to flake off quietly along the way, and hopefully just disappear.

Perhaps there was insufficient money to cater to anyone beyond the majority, but the explanation probably was not quite that innocent. The equally potent reason for this stance was that Winterset, and untold towns like her, wanted to safe-guard its image of normality. The kids growing up in our town were certain to contribute to society in just the same format as had their parents and more distant ancestors. Any renegades or ingrates would just have to fend for themselves. Certainly the school budget was not going to encourage veering off the sanctioned path.

Thus a section of the high school building was devoted to what girls were expected to become. A big room/rooms (?) full of ovens, sinks, and cutting blocks. I'm guessing a bit as you can tell, because I never set foot in this bastion of femininity.

There was also a section, on the opposite corner, devoted to what boys obviously wanted to do with any hobby time life would offer—a big woodworking studio, called "shop," full of table saws and other accoutrements needed to learn how to repair cabinets and otherwise keep a household in good working order. The girls did not set foot in this room.

But the girls were *required* to habitate the 'home-economics' section; classes there were mandatory for them at least to some minimum degree. And the boys were likewise required to spend at least one semester in the 'shop.' It did not matter a whit whether the student was interested in, or had any remote aptitude in the area of work involved. It was just a Winterset given. The idea of a female not being handy in the kitchen, or a male without a basement workshop, were simply outside the range of Winterset's imagination.

If you were female you needed to be able to cook, and if you were male you needed to be able to hammer and saw. Life, after all, was simple and we knew our assigned roles from the beginning. Whatever 'boys will be boys' might imply outside the class room, within the school system it meant compliance to the expected norm. No one was allowed to escape, at least without going through the motions.

But life was not really as simple as the school board wanted to believe. I can't speak for the girls, but I can for some of the boys. I just wasn't very

# Tuesday

good at my assigned role of mechanic and builder, nor were some of my classmates.

A little knot of us at the beginning of the semester selected building a birdhouse as our 'shop' project, although many of our peers set their sights on far grander, more complicated, projects. I struggled mightily. By the end of the semester my birdhouse was still not finished and I earned the worst mark of my high school career—worse even than in algebra which I never understood to the slightest degree. And as I recall, there were a couple of other unfinished birdhouses in the room as well. I was, it would seem, the very opposite of my father and brother, both wizzes at making useful things out of a few scraps of wood. Or of my grandfather who built several Winterset houses by hand as a retirement hobby.

For me, 'shop' was alien territory. The trouble was, I was required to spend at least a semester there. Surely that semester would turn me into a more satisfactory version of a small town male. It didn't.

It's revealing, I think, that no option was given for co-ed use of either of these high school resources. I believe in time the thinking may have changed, but in my day the idea that a boy could be interested in cooking or a girl in construction was not only dismissed out of hand, it was strictly forbidden as a possible besmirchment to the purity of life as practiced in Winterset.

The idea that a local boy, or probably any boy for that matter, could have someday emerged as a famous chef, or that any local girl might have turned into a Sally Ride, was apparently not within the imaginative grasp of our school officials. They knew without question what boys and girls were headed for, and they felt the obligation also to enforce that vision to the extent they could. What had been good enough for boys and girls for decades was still good enough for them.

We were still in a "boys don't cry" era where life was supposed to unfold along safe and stereotypical lines. It didn't always. But the individuals for whom it didn't were expected to be quiet about it, and not to ruffle the waters—not to challenge the certainty that the boys and girls of Winterset were of the most mainstream and wholesome mien possible.

While trying to adequately prepare its students for adulthood, and doing so I have no doubt in the most sincere way possible, the schools were inadvertently enforcing the limitations of a small town perspective on life. Our wings were being clipped a bit. Our horizons were being held in check. We were being prepared to fill the next generation needed for Winterset to carry on as usual. Variations on the theme, after all, would have meant nothing but trouble. And small towns in Iowa were not about to enable any trouble-making paid for by tax dollars. ⌘

# 16 Wednesday
## Highways Through the Centers of Towns

During my childhood family vacations were an exercise in frugality (our parents were still recovering from the war). If we stayed anywhere commercially, it was in a cheap roadside motel and we ate a picnic which Mom had prepared in advance and brought along. Mostly, however, both for my family and many other families at the time as well, 'vacation' meant visiting relatives and staying with them.

For my brother and me, Mendota, Illinois, played the biggest 'vacation' role in our childhood. Not for its attractions, but because we had relatives to stay with. My dad had all manner of relatives in the Mendota area from both his father's and his mother's side. He and one of his first cousins, Harry, were evidently closer than was the case with his other cousins there, so we descended on Harry and his family with some frequency.

Harry had inherited his father's farm just outside Mendota and lived and worked there with two sons approximately the ages of my brother and me. These boys had their own pony, which we'd hitch up to a wagon to ride around the farm, and they had access to all kinds of interesting things and animals which we town boys found diverting. Inside the large farm house, these boys also had their very own downstairs room which they'd filled with various games and lots and lots of comic books.

I was in their room reading comic books on the late side of one evening; the other three boys had gone off to bed upstairs but I'd lingered to further my literary education. Then, unexpectedly, I got another of my little bits of birds and bees education which I was stringing together trying to form a whole.

The grown-ups were in their living room (parlor?) next to the boys' comic books room. I was engrossed in my funny book and hardly paying attention to the adult conversation. But all of a sudden the adult's words began to slice through the hall. "Yes, but that first night after the wedding…..?" Another voice, with a hint of mild panic, "Have the boys

# Wednesday

gone to bed yet?" This was my signal to disappear, I could tell. So I left my book and headed upstairs, always wanting to be seen as a "good boy" even at the expense of not hearing what surely seemed to be heading in an interesting direction among the adults.

These "vacations" (vacations for us at least, although I'm not sure how much that was the case for Harry and his wife) usually took us for a picnic to the near-by Starved Rock State Park. This was the site where settlers of yore apparently drove a tribe of native Americans up onto a large rocky hill and starved them away, rather than simply shooting them away. In any case the Indians came to no good end. The history of such a disgrace didn't really interest me much at that age, but the park had several refreshment stands and souvenir shops which lent it a festive atmosphere appealing even to a school-boy.

The most exotic vacation trip during my childhood was a rail trip to Buffalo, New York, with a midnight stopover in Detroit offering the chance to walk into Cadillac Square at night. As always, though, the parameters were set by frugality. There was absolutely no thought of a hotel stop in Detroit. The trip was straight through with whatever sleep one could grab on the train. And the destination was another home-stay, with my mother's brother and his family.

That said, this trip probably echoed the currently stereotypical idea of Americans on vacation more than our Illinois excursions. Nearby, easily within day-trip parameters, was one of the country's great tourist attractions: Niagara Falls. So we did the tourist circuit there, we kids bought a few cheap souvenirs, and we all dined on a picnic from my aunt's kitchen to avoid any further undue costs.

Beyond that I can recall only three other family vacations during boyhood. One was a driving trip to Colorado shared with my Dad's newly widowed father, again with roadside picnics along the way in order to avoid the profligacy of restaurant dining. This had been preceded by an earlier Colorado trip where we stayed with my mother's widowed aunt and saw several old mining towns converted into colorful tourist traps. And before that, a visit to this same aunt in a little town in South Dakota celebrating its centennial with a big parade.

There is one further glimmer of a family vacation faintly holding on to a wisp of memory, the faintness of the image owing to my delicate age at the time. I could not have been older than four or five, and am not even sure if my brother was on the scene by then; if so, he was still a pre-ambulatory infant.

My parents had rented a cabin on a fishing lake in northern Iowa and rented a row boat to go with it. The cabin was set in a long row of identical bland white two-room buildings facing the lake. Everyday my father would venture out onto the lake and return late afternoon with a string of fish. My mother then set about cleaning the fish and preparing to serve them for dinner.

I don't think I got even a single trip over the water, being still practically a baby myself, but I do have one of those vivid snippets of memory which provide small snapshots of very early childhood. Weirdly it is of another boy urinating. Staying in one of the other cabins was a boy about my age with whom I spent most of the week. Once when he needed to relieve himself we walked between two of the closely spaced cabins and he peed against the side of one of them; a pretty standard kind of childhood memory most likely. But I was riveted by how white his urine was. Not the slightest golden hue that I could detect. And somehow a rather bizarre memory to stay with me all these years.

We were living in an age of travel prior to President Eisenhower and his Interstate Highway system, so travel by highway was not only a longer process than it would be just a few years hence, but these highways actually still cut through the hearts of real towns along the way. This made driving much more interesting than seeing huge endless fields of corn, attractive as the corn was to Iowa eyes.

One of the largest towns along our route to Illinois was Iowa City, my university town-in-waiting. On return trips the highway took us right to the heart of the town and placed us on a section of Iowa Avenue as it headed directly toward the Old Capitol building, Iowa's first statehouse.

I was by then a big fan of absorbing Iowa history, mostly by reading from that section of the Winterset public library. So when, on one particular return trip from Illinois, I saw this great building looming before us, I started begging my dad to stop so we could walk around and see the building up close. My dad was driving, as always, probably already exhausted by then, and I was sitting in the front seat between him and his sister, my Aunt Ina. "Please, please stop, Dad," I begged as he drove relentlessly, and silently, onward. My reaction to the still moving car was to throw a pout, perhaps enlivened with a few school-boy words like, "You never do anything I want."

My aunt took it upon herself to defend her brother. "Your parents do lots for you," she began a somewhat longer lecture to me. I decided to punish all of them; I would not speak another word for at least a few weeks. I sat there, squeezed between my father and my aunt, sulking and absolutely silent, and hoping they were absorbing the full brunt of my righteous indignation. A few more interesting little towns graced our route and I gradually forgot I was punishing them. My boycott of family life didn't last quite as long as I'd planned.

Later, as a university student, that old Iowa Statehouse at the center of campus, would become familiar and beloved territory for me. I still thrill at seeing it on return visits. On its front limestone steps early in my time in Iowa City I stood with a previously unexperienced pride at a pep rally before the start of football season—Iowa was ranked, as I recall, number one in the country and the sense of hitting the big time was an invigorating joy for a small town guy like me. Unfortunately, the number one ranking disappeared rather quickly that season, the first for head coach Jerry Burns who had just replaced the legendary Forest Evashevski.

But walking to football games, from the main campus over to the medical campus and the stadium, brought another sort of thrill for me. I was still a bit of a nut job on Iowa history, and chauvinistic beyond reason. I'd pause briefly on the bridge over the river to recite to myself the geography of being, at that moment, at the very heart of the universe. I was standing in the most 'Iowa" place available to mankind: On Iowa Avenue, crossing the Iowa River, on the campus of the University of Iowa, in Iowa City, Iowa. It just did not get any more Iowa than that.

And Iowa seemed plenty. Somewhere along the way in my early high school years, Aunt Ina and Uncle Scotty took me along on a trip to Chicago, by Greyhound bus. So I had an idea of what things might be like outside Iowa, but they were never a siren call—at least until graduate school when I landed in Philadelphia by happenstance and my horizons were forced to widen. Until then Iowa was all I could wish for. In many ways it still is. I would have loved to have spent some of my adult years in Iowa City or Des Moines had circumstances allowed. And even now I sometimes daydream about moving back to Winterset for my last few years. In these dreams I usually open a wonderful little boutique restaurant on the Square, with outside dining in the summer and another little trace of Paris in Winterset.

## GERMANY, BRITAIN, IOWA

My father had grown up in Alabama, on a farm outside Mobile, so he and the houseful of my relatives across the street in Winterset had experienced at least a bit of the wider world. If it marked them in any way, however, the difference was indistinguishable to me. They seemed just like every other Iowan I knew of, which may simply have been because everyone's roots there were ultimately rural.

As I grew I did have periods of curiosity about who my people were and where they came from.

My dad's family was solidly of German descent so there was not much mystery to speculate about on that front. It was fairly obvious from family conversations that these German-Americans grouped together in colonies. And then they routinely married within those German colonies so there had been little chance for other nationalistic influences to color our tribe.

My dad's father was a member of the first generation of his family born in this country rather than Germany; and my dad was from the first generation of his family not able to speak fluent German but still having a small cocktail conversation vocabulary in the language when needed (which might have been over beers, but never cocktails). Even that small toehold in German was lost with my generation, probably because the only foreign language study choice in the Winterset school system was Spanish.

When the Truckenbrods emigrated from Germany they had settled mostly in Illinois where they became farmers, following in the footsteps of their ancestors. Some ended up in the Buffalo, New York, area and a few others in Texas, although I have no idea whether they split off from the Illinois colony or represented separate waves of immigration. The founder of the Illinois Truckenbrods was my great grandfather John who was born in Bavaria and had fourteen children with my great grandmother Elizabeth who was born in Saxe-Coburg.

My dad's mother was from the Illinois clan of Gross, so her Germanic credentials were in solid order as well. The Illinois Gross colony had spawned a satellite colony in Adair County Iowa centered in the miniscule town of Fontanelle. The biggest building in Fontanelle was the Lutheran church which served the local Germans, including my grandmother's large clan of brothers and their families. Therefore, my dad's family was just recently American and had not been here long enough to get into much trouble on the genetic variation front.

Later in life as a newspaper arts reporter I learned I had a colleague in Pittsburgh named Druckenbrod, so the original Truckenbrod immigrants may have adapted in ways which made them less easy to trace than one might have expected. I gather that the various people with variants of the name were at least distantly related but none were siblings of the John Truckenbrod who immigrated in 1834 to found our specific tribe. (If you're curious, by the way, the name appears to mean "dry bread," as in bread eaten without butter. It should be pronounced with a long "o" since it was derived from Truckenbrodt, with the final "t" dropped. No one outside our family ever pronounced it that way, however. They always added an "a" after the "o" and confidently changed the pronunciation to match.)

My mother's family tree was not even easy to guess about except for the obviously British family names. The first, and biggest, problem is that they

## Wednesday

had been here so long that the possible variations which could have entered the picture were uncountable—they may very well have come over on the Mayflower for all anyone knew. To me they seemed like the sort of people who would not have been very adventuresome in their choice of mates, so I assumed that my mother's people were basically English, or at least British, as their names testified. My grandfather had the solidly British (likely Welch) family name Roberts, and my grandmother was a Garrett, originally a Norman name but transplanted to England long before any Brits thought about moving to America.

One of my mother's aunts did become interested in genealogy, as seemed to happen frequently with the childless members of big families, and she made a hobby of trying to map out a family tree. She traced the family in this country back to the flag-maker Betsy Ross, giving us solid American colonial credentials. Her detective work on the European side suggested we were descended from the royal House of Orange in Holland, and thus also had some distant connection with the British royals after William of Orange.

Interesting, in an abstract way, as all of this was, it never satisfied my curiosity about the more recent American generations of my mother's people. I was left to assume they were plain vanilla, as their Methodist ties suggested. My cousin Jimmy came up with one small monkey-wrench to throw into this perspective, however. He was convinced for some reason that our Grandpa Roberts had engaged in an affair of the heart somewhere along the way after he married our grandmother. As unlikely as this seemed to me, it did open the possibility that maybe my mother's side of the family had been a touch more adventuresome than I gave them credit for being. Maybe, despite appearances, there was a hint of exotic blood in our veins after all.

So it was that my dad's side of the family seemed the more foreign and therefore the more exotic. Not that either side really offered much exotic appeal. But although I would go through life with an unmistakably German name, as life unfurled it was my mother's ancestral background which exerted the greatest appeal and held the most sway for me. I ended up travelling frequently in the UK, both for business and for sheer appeal and cultural affinity.

In Germany not so much—only twice. Once just by walking across a bridge from Switzerland and quickly exploring the business area of a rusty old town of no apparent distinction. And once just to get to someplace else, by train from Denmark on the way to France with one overnight hotel stay. But it may have been a colorful stop-over. There was some frustration about the room we were assigned, and evidently my request for a change turned into a bit of a shouting match at the registration counter. My now husband tells me I got heated to the point that I shouted at the clerk, "I'm more German than you are!" Ludicrous as that was, if "German" were translated as "stubborn," as it sometimes was in folklore, I may have been correct in my evaluation.

England on the other hand seemed almost like home. And my work as an agent for performing musicians and choirs gave me entrée into the spiritual essence of the place and the race. I got to eat many meals in the actual private homes of Englishmen of a wide variety of stripes and means. And I had access to the inner workings of famous schools like Eton, Trinity College, and Christ Church. Add to that John's Scottish roots, which we did explore geographically as well, and the UK was perhaps our home away from home—challenged only by France. Whether we have visited England or France more frequently is a statistic lost in the clouds of many happy decades, and with Italy beginning to wage its own claim to the title.

And then of course, being Iowans my family could also toss in a little honorary French heritage from this side of the Atlantic too—Louisiana Purchase, Dubuque, Des Moines—so we were safely part of the great American melting pot. All of us, the country over, gradually dropping the geographical and ethnic adjectives and thinking of ourselves increasingly as just "Americans."

I was sure about the Iowa part of it in any case. We were Iowans, and farmers, from many generations back. My mother's parents were the first to leave the farm for a life, and business, in town—a gas filling station with a little motel in the slightly smaller than Winterset town of Greenfield. But my brother and I were the first generation actually born into town life; the first generation to have no personal roots on the farm, or *per se* in Iowa's rich black soil.

Actually, I was the first individual member of my extended family not to grow up on a farm and could lay claim to being the first actual town kid of the lot; to the best of my knowledge also the first to be born in town rather than on the farm (in my grandparents' house; hospitals had not yet sprung up in many Iowa county seat towns although most had a doctor's office or two with backrooms used for minor surgery. Babies, however, were still generally delivered at home by midwives. Or, as in my case, by grandmothers).

My cousin Jimmy, just behind me in the birth sequence of our generation, trumped me by being born in a big city in the urban East (Buffalo, New York, although not involving the Buffalo Truckenbrods I presume), and probably in a hospital. For him, visits to Winterset and

## Wednesday

Greenfield were probably as exotic as visits to my other grandparents' farm were for me.

If I was in the vanguard of anything by just being, it would have been as part of Iowa's very gradual transition from mostly rural to mostly urban. For me life on the farm could be observed but was not experienced. The family farm was still the dominant part of the folkloric romance of the place, of its legends, its ethos, and even its customs. But Iowans were gradually becoming city people (or at least town people). And there I was—part of a gradual but deep demographic shift, maybe not from my own merits or efforts, but a trend-setter nonetheless. ⌘

*Shades of New England, one of Madison County's famous covered bridges (photo: Teddi Yaeger)*

# 17 Thursday
## Beware Yellow Unless it Flies

Thursday was the week's most malleable day. It meant school, of course, but otherwise it didn't seem to have a specific shape or direction. Not that it was stuck in the middle of the school week; that was Wednesday's job. But it was not fresh like Monday nor full of anticipation like Friday. Thursday was just sort of hanging around marking time.

By about third or fourth grade, however, Thursday did acquire a fragment of distinction. A couple of the boys started to circulate the discovery by one of them that yellow clothing was to be assiduously avoided on this day.

The reasons for this fashion regimen were rather hazy, as were so many of life's discoveries at that stage, although they seemed to involve primarily the avoidance of being recognized as a "sissy."

Maybe it was even more than that; maybe yellow actually *conferred* sissyhood on the wearer if the calendar said Thursday. While I use the sissy word here, a somewhat more robust word pointing in a similar direction was used by a few of the boys as they educated us on the recently discovered clothing codes. Whatever the case, yellow and Thursday were suddenly a forbidden combination.

So I never dressed in yellow on a Thursday, even though I wasn't totally sure what being a sissy was all about beyond the obvious conclusion that one was not supposed to want to be recognized as one. Nor did I quite understand why some guys would want to advertise their sissy-ness by saving their yellow shirt for Thursdays. Best to play it safe in case being a sissy, or being recognized as one, was as bad as it sounded.

And another mystery left unsolved was why Thursday was any different from any other day on the sissy front. It was okay, apparently, to wear yellow on Monday, for example, although I decided I'd best play it safe by eliminating yellow entirely from my closet.

So Thursdays could mean anything. Maybe it had been on Thursdays, years earlier, that we tiny scholars had lined up in the basement gloom of the North Ward grade school to be inoculated against whatever disease the authorities wanted to protect us from at the moment. Maybe it was on Thursdays that the teachers got together to compare notes about their little charges.

Nothing was really certain about Thursdays, although my guess is that one saw very little yellow on the playground other than maybe on the girls—girls seemed to live by different rules than did the boys. Maybe girls were not liable to being mistaken for sissies, and therefore could dress in a wash of yellow if they wanted. Come to think of it, maybe girls *were* sissies by natural selection or divine right. Maybe that was the whole reason the boys had to demonstrate on Thursdays that they were not color blind. (This was the Winterset version of the yellow/Thursday thing at least; some historians of classical mythology might argue that it was the girls who should have eschewed yellow rather than the boys.)

The only firm conclusion one could draw from all of this was that by fourth grade there were boys, and there were girls, and that the two mixed like oil and water. That, and also that for a boy to retain his budding masculine honor he at least had to avoid yellow on Thursdays whatever the true underlying reason.

By early high school people started to wear yellow if they wanted to, regardless of the calendar. That may not have meant that the threat of being regarded as, or recognized as, a sissy had been entirely eliminated. And by then there was quite a bit less mystery involved in what being a sissy entailed; although it had acquired along the way some darker tones which still didn't exactly have their own specific names yet in 1956 in a place like Winterset, despite the linguistic pioneering efforts of the boys back in fourth grade. But at least it was easier by then to guess how a sissy might behave, so everyone had the advantage of the key to community acceptance—just act exactly like everyone else. Conformity and uniformity became the sacraments of life in high school.

At the same time, perhaps ironically, our personal worlds were expanding, and we were beginning to understand that not everyone really is alike despite our adolescent aspirations in that direction. There were going to be all kinds of people populating our worlds, and instead of being threatening, that was beginning to hint at an intriguing variety of experience. We were beginning to be a little more cosmopolitan even though we still lived in a small and somewhat insulated Midwestern town.

## BIRDS OF A DARING YELLOW

By early high school, too, we were being challenged to look around and notice our context. Taking up that challenge with gusto, I decided to make my science class project finding out how many species of birds inhabited or passed through our area; to find out by direct observation rather than reading a book. This, evidently, was what science is about, even though my project already had a commonly used name: "bird watching."

For months I would get up much earlier in the morning than I actually needed in order to get ready for school, and I'd venture out with a pair of binoculars to search the trees of our yard, of our neighborhood, and as the project mushroomed, of the whole town. Then my mother became intrigued and joined the hunt. She would drive me out to the town park or into the vast stretches of farmland and we'd note down all the varieties of birds we could identify visually and audibly. Autumn turned into winter and still we persevered, collecting data that rewarded its collection by the triumph of spotting more and more species. (And for what it's worth, many of those species were proudly, unabashedly, yellow, even on Thursdays.)

The project had to become tangible in order to get a grade, so I collected all of our data into a three-ring binder. Each bird species had its own page upon which I'd paste a photo or painting of the particular bird and some general info about its range. Then I carefully listed each sighting of that species: date, time, location. By the next semester life had rushed on, as always, and new challenges had nearly obliterated my bird-watching memories.

Our high school principal, H.C. Miller, was a very difficult character to read. On the surface he was stiff, formal, and maybe a touch gruff. Yet his interest in his students, their well-being, and their progress was obvious. He seemed almost a cross between a bull-dog and a mother hen. He seemed like a Marine Sargent and something deep in my memory suggests that the image may have had some connection to his reality. He cared about his students, but sometimes one had to look past a surface formality to understand that. He was, in fact, a very proud father watching carefully over his flock but always very careful not to appear sentimental in the process.

Mr. Miller at the end of the school day always left his office and perched off to the side at the top of the wide staircase to watch his students leave the building. This ritual was usually silent—just a protective father-figure watching carefully as his charges temporarily retreated from his care and returned to the world, or at least to their biological parents.

## Thursday

One second semester afternoon as I reached the stairs to begin my descent to the streets of Winterset, Mr. Miller held out his arm to block my way. In his hand was the binder I had assembled from my science class bird watching endeavors. If he said anything it was a brief word or two which I don't remember now. But his usually inscrutable face betrayed a bit of paternal pride and just the merest hint of a smile. I took the notebook and (hopefully) thanked him. I descended the stairs feeling the glow of words I don't believe he actually uttered, but I knew he fully intended: "Job well done." ⌘

# 18 Friday Like the Other Boys

My Winterset school days seemed littered with failed attempts to be like the other guys, and of course during those years there is almost nothing more important to a boy than fitting in. As much as I tried I was never very good at it, and at the time I couldn't figure out whether that resulted from personal inadequacies or some kind of grand flaw with humanity. It always felt like the first and thus always sent me out with a little cloud of frustration and slight shame hovering around my head.

One warm summer day after I'd pulled the mower out of the garage getting ready for my lawn duty, I just decided I was tired of being swallowed up in clothing head-to-toe like some kind of Lutheran nun. It was a gorgeous sun-drenched day and the humidity of summer was already placing itself in sticky evidence. So on an atypical impulse I found an old pair of jeans and cut the legs off. Then I went about my assigned duty of mowing our lawn in a previously unexperienced freedom of movement and mood.

My new summer uniform did feel perhaps a touch odd; I was as white as paper, having no tan below my neck or hands, and the feel of the breeze on my hither-to-concealed skin was an unusual, but pleasant and somehow newly masculine, sensation—maybe even a bit daring since I rarely had shed even my shirt outside. But at least I felt a bit more like one of the boys for a few minutes. I was wearing just sneakers, socks, and my new cut-offs. I was somehow engaging with life in a new and somewhat exciting way; a way which seemed to imitate the script a lot of my peers followed routinely.

My Grandpa used to walk from his house across the street from ours, and down the alley to visit my dad's machine shop, at least once a day. I was mowing the front lawn when I saw him set out, crossing the street at his late-seventies pace. But this time he headed directly toward me instead of the alley. When he arrived I shut down the mower so he could speak, and so I could hear him.

"A little much, don't ya think?" he announced, not really asking my opinion as his words themselves might have implied, but rendering the verdict instantly. The judgement was already in; my response was not needed nor called for, except to correct my indiscretion. I knew we were Germans by descent, but wow, maybe some Amish had gotten mixed in along the way. Maybe his objection was because we weren't on the farm anymore; maybe life in town called for a stricter dignity than I'd observed in some of my peers' dress codes after all. The only possible infraction I could think I might have been guilty of was possibly having made the shorts a little too short, but even so they covered more territory than the swim trunks of the day and those never seemed to raise an eyebrow.

Now, my grandpa didn't seem to me like the sort of man who would venture into such waters voluntarily, any more than would his son, my dad. In our family this sort of policing and enforcement was women's work, and I suspected my grandma was surveying the scene from behind the sheer curtains of her window across the street, having dispatched her husband to deliver the verdict, albeit without much enthusiasm on his part. He had paused no more than a second or two before setting out on his true mission of walking up to the machine shop.

Any fragment of "coming of age" tension I can recall always pivoted on what my mother's reaction would be, never what my father's reaction would be. He didn't react to matters of this sort. That was his wife's job, and they seem to have had a firmly worked out agreement to that effect.

It was not only the police work that the females of my family were in charge of. I began to suspect that religion in general was part of their official portfolio as well.

Although Lutheranism ran in our blood from German fountains, the men who passed on the German name and traditions could be rather indifferent to the Sunday by Sunday practice of their official religion. It was the women who insisted on church attendance every single Sunday, or whenever there might be an extra service such as on Wednesdays during Lent, and it was the men who went along with the idea silently. But the men also took a little vacation from this obligation every so often at their discretion. I could not tell if this small latitude was part of the official arrangement, or if the women grudgingly tolerated it because they could not control the adult men as effectively as they could control the boys.

My mother, with the legendary zeal of the convert (she had grown up a Methodist, although only her father bothered to attend church services; not her more liberated mother), for a long period of years insisted that my brother and I listen to her read from a devotional book every morning before we left for school. Even I, the religious goody-two-shoes of my generation, got really weary of these "devotions" and began to find them a little embarrassing on top of that.

Anyway, evidence that most boys in town of my age observed a different summer dress-code than the Lutheran version was fairly easy to discover—just open one's eyes. But for young Phil it was dutifully back into the closet, safe again for Lutheran eyes to happen upon. Knowing I'd never be able to wear the newly fashioned cut-offs again, into the trash they went.

Wanting to be just one of the boys was sort of a frustration which hovered above me throughout my school days. I just wasn't very good at it, and often enough didn't even quite understand what it was supposed to entail.

I certainly had figured out that I was supposed be crazy about sports and to be spending all my free time enthusiastically playing baseball as did so many of by peers. But inside I knew I wasn't an athlete and had to admit to myself that I actually hated baseball—or any other kind of 'ball' for that matter. Actually, I didn't really possess sufficient coordination to even catch one of the damn things until I was an adult, which was pretty unhandy since I had to spend my childhood in the outfield praying that no one would hit a ball in my direction.

And if someone *were* so inconsiderate as to hit a ball in my direction I then had to face the humiliation of demonstrating before God and man that I couldn't throw it back more than a few feet. And that was always well short of getting it back inside the diamond—and that is also perhaps why a clever base runner had inevitably hit one in my direction in the first place. This, in turn, made me the official "last one chosen" whenever teams were picked on the playground, nearly the scarlet letter of boyhood and a distinction I had to endure until advancing grades finally gave me opportunities to engineer avoiding the playground altogether.

Perhaps it's some kind of grand irony that such a kid would grow up to become absolutely bananas about University of Iowa football and eager to fly across the country almost every season for at least one game. But then the gods are full of little surprises along the way. (By the way, later in life at a cocktail party in New York I met a guy who claimed he was Nile Kinnick's roommate at Iowa, but I'm not sure I believed him—that's just too good to be true.)

So I went through grade school worried that I might be a "sissy," and that possibility had probably occurred to a few people around me as well. Fortunately I never got a really detailed definition of what being a sissy entailed, so I was free to rationalize my inadequacies. I preferred to think that my ongoing failures to be just one of the boys had more to do with being a "good" boy than being a sissy boy. I liked that explanation a lot better. I'm not sure if the adults around me always thought of me as a good

## Friday

boy, but I certainly did—it was the refuge that gave me the courage to step into each new day.

And I had a lofty reason for being good as well as a self-protective one. I'd known since at least second grade that I wanted to become a clergyman. Certainly clergymen were "good;" the very epitome of good evidently. So I threw myself into the business of being good. This gave me some cover for my boyish inadequacies; it kept the adults, if not my peers, off the scent of my possibly also being a sissy, or at least I hoped it did.

But even for a 'good' boy the definition of being 'just one of the boys' kept taking on new meanings and complications as we climbed the ladder of school grades. And organized religion didn't seem to help very much in fending them off. Being just one of the boys, or wanting to be, was a shifting ground under my feet as grade school yielded to early high school.

At about age fifteen I signed up for a weeklong church event called "Leadership Training School," or words close to that, in which the cream of Iowa Lutheran young people were gathered to be helped along their ways to becoming church big-wigs of the future, although actually anyone at all could sign up for it. It might also be noted that the classes were simply the same old Bible lessons and pep-talks on being 'good' that we got at home, so I don't think I actually advanced toward church leadership in any revelatory way.

I had talked my boyhood friend Keith into joining me in this righteous educational endeavor and he and I were roommates at this affair, dutifully attending every class and session and keeping a low and godly profile in our cabin.

But things were more interesting in the cabin's other room which three guys shared. Every day they played a game designed to see which of them could shoot the farthest as they watched some of the girls on a nearby playground. Every day I desperately wanted to go into their room as the games heated up; every day I thought I'd like to challenge their distance markings. But we were training to become Lutheran leaders. How could I bend to such un-Christian activity?

On the final day I actually did walk in, and one of the guys cheerily called out, "I knew we'd get old Phil in here one of these days." I'd been welcomed warmly—but the games had petered out for the day, and I was left as not like the other boys as seemed always to be the case, but at least still unchallenged in the "good" department.

Trying to convince myself, and to please the adults around me, by being "good" definitely did not add up to being "just one of the boys." And especially so as life kept escalating the definition of what 'boys being boys' might entail. ⌘

# 19 Saturday On the Town

Saturday had a catch-all flavor to it which gave it an excitement uniquely its own. Tomorrow, Sunday, most of the stores would be closed and a calm would settle in. Saturday was the day to shop for the weekend, and probably for the whole week, especially if one lived on a farm and made just one trip into town per week. Saturday evening, as a result, was the commercial magnet of the week. It was a day feeling the pressure of needing to get things wrapped up and squared away.

Saturday felt the bustle of life more than any of its sibling days. Unless perhaps, one were still a younger schoolboy and free to escape to the matinee screening at the Iowa movie theater on the town Square where John Wayne, Roy Rogers, and Gene Autry were the heroes of the day.

Saturday was also the day to prepare for church on Sunday; for me at least, although I suspect very few of my peers shared that particular perspective. My job for years was to help our pastor run off the Sunday church 'bulletins,' essentially event programs, on our manual crank mimeograph machine.

The job itself was simple in the extreme. He would crank out the bulletins and I would insert after each one issued forth a buffer sheet designed to soak up enough ink to prevent the actual bulletins from imprinting on each other. How I came to be entrusted with this obviously important task is lost to history at this point, but it was an easy job which I was not capable of screwing up, and equally obviously, I was busy doing the Lord's work which meant my mother approved whole heartedly.

While as a boy I never questioned anything having to do with church, there was nonetheless a hint of mystery about these church bulletins, given to each worshipper as s/he entered for the Sunday service. The mystery which was just beginning to flit through my pint-sized brain was why were they needed in the first place?

There were three aspects to these mini-booklets formed by folding a standard stationary sized sheet of paper in half. First off, the side which became the face cover and the back cover were pre-printed in color. They were prepared by and ordered from denominational sources. They normally followed the liturgical year except during the long, dry "Trinity season" when they could wander off in whatever direction the editors fancied. Okay, I guess these covers had a useful function—they helped keep us on seasonal track and they augmented the religious messages issuing forth from the pulpit.

Inside, on the right facing page, locally produced by the pastor on his typewriter while cutting the stencil, was a series of bits of information, news, prayer requests for ill parish members, etc. This page was a touch more mysterious than the printed covers because the service itself always had a big space allotted to "announcements" where this type of thing seemed to belong, and where indeed it was usually repeated vocally in any case. Maybe we were setting the stage in case a deaf person should happen into our service and could not hear the oral announcements. Or maybe some of our older church members were harder of hearing than I realized as a mere lad, and they needed to see what they might have difficulty hearing. Okay again. This page had a potentially useful function.

*Iowa theater on the East side of the Winterset Square (photo: Teddi Yaeger)*

The real mystery, for me, was the inside front cover page. Here was always a list of the various set liturgical components which constituted the Lutheran service, together with the page number in the hymnal where one could find this little segment printed out. Now, the Lutheran 'service' was essentially Mass, although no one would have dreamed of using, or dared to use, that title. We would usually call it 'Holy Communion' or perhaps 'the Eucharist' if one were a little more ecclesiastically oriented, but whatever the title it had to be diluted just enough that it didn't seem too 'Catholic' (heaven forfend!). Whatever we were, we were emphatically not Catholics.

But it was Mass whether we called it that or not, although we Lutherans had chopped it into two pieces, and on a routine Sunday would stop half way through and go home. It was only about once a month when the whole ritual would be performed. Perhaps this was another way of insuring that we didn't look too much like the Catholics, who went for broke every Sunday over on their side of town.

The Catholics, bless them, had solved this problem eons ago by either memorizing the order and responses of Mass (still in Latin at that point) or by bringing along a missal which they could follow. Nothing ever varied except specific prayers and responses needed for a particular liturgical season anyway, in either church. And the Lutherans didn't even have to remember to bring along a missal. Right in front of them, in the rack which held the hymnals, was waiting a complete blow-by-blow account of what would be spoken (never sung or intoned in those days) by the pastor, and what the people should say or sing in response, segment by segment. The Lutherans, in effect, had their missals right in front of their noses.

Even so, evidently they also needed a play-by-play listing with page references so they could follow along, with or without the hymnal. This, to me, was a mystery, although of course I never hinted at my confusion to the pastor while he cranked out the Sunday bulletins. I remained loyal to what, surely, must have a perfectly cogent, and pious, explanation without a clue as to what the explanation was. These good folks in the pews had been attending these services long before I was born and each Sunday the *Angus Dei* had landed in exactly the same place and was expressed in exactly the same words as it had on every previous Sunday. Was I the only one in church who had figured that out?

I pictured the Lutherans at their dinner tables all week long worried that suddenly next Sunday the *Sanctus* would be moved to a different place in the line-up. There was no point in leaving folks to bear that kind of stress, so we kept publishing the weekly bulletin with its reassuring list of Mass segments militantly in exactly the same order they had been in every week as long as anyone could remember. It was part of the pastor's job, evidently, to both reassure the faithful and to clue them in to any new wrinkles in the liturgy—of which there never were any, of course.

Regardless of whatever rationalities were, or were not, involved I faithfully kept doing my part to put a sheet of paper in the hands of every Sunday morning Lutheran. Then the person would not be too surprised that the creed was going to land in a particular place in the ceremony. Maybe life was simpler for the Presbyterians or the Methodists, but I never bothered to explore that possibility.

Anyway, Saturday evening would wipe away any continuing confusion over church bulletins. Saturday evening was fiesta time. If there were going to be a traffic jam anywhere in Winterset's week, it would take place around the Square on Saturday evening. Car horns might even be employed, although more in greeting and good will than impatience.

Everyone from miles around had left their farms for a night on the town, even though for most of them I suspect it amounted to little more than shopping for groceries with overflowing carts. My role in this happy mayhem evolved with age, from enthralled observer, to being a grocery bagger and carry-out boy, to an actual clerk selling clothing directly to farm wives at the J.C. Penney store. Winterset on a Saturday evening was almost a big-city, and I was in my element.

By Saturday evening the movie theater had put away the afternoon cowboy flicks and moved on to some film of current appeal which brought in a full house. Its wonderful neon marquee presided over a scene of an almost urban flavor, and I have no doubt welcomed many young couples into its dimly lit embrace. As I very gradually became aware, nature had placed that sort of burden on me only in the lightest and most theoretical of ways, so my career of "necking" with a girl in the Iowa Theater was limited to a handful of times I could probably count on just one of my hands. And in any case, on Saturday evenings I was gainfully employed and thus had an explanation for resisting such temptations of the flesh, and this saved me from worrying about the situation too much. Winterset was sufficiently exciting quite on its own on a Saturday evening. ⌘

# 20 Leap Year Bonus Day

If the ancient gods of the prairie granted me one day to return to the Winterset of my childhood, I think I'd choose to be somewhere close to age twelve and in the sixth grade. Things were starting to get a little more interesting and complicated (read "girls") with just a hint of looming adulthood, but we had not yet been expelled from the simple joys of having very few expectations engulfing us. There was increasing freedom without increasing responsibilities, although those responsibilities were waiting for us just around a corner we didn't realize we'd be soon obligated to turn.

It wouldn't be a school day, although I loved school at that point. We were in the top class of the North Ward School and our teacher was the Principal, Mr. Bectal. He treated us like we were already adults, and talked to us as though we were wise enough to understand what he was talking about. He'd often sit on the edge of his big desk that faced our rows of individual desks, now each with a small storage capacity if the desk-top was lifted up like a lid, and he would just talk to us.

It might have been merely a stream-of-conscientious monologue, but I couldn't tell with certainty and I didn't know what that term would have meant yet anyway. But he talked to us about current events and grown-up stuff like he might have expected us to know something about. It felt like we were being liberated from the six levels of schooling that had comprised most of our life experience to date. It felt like we were the Seniors of North Ward, although we'd soon have to move on to a new school where we'd once again need to start at the bottom of the ladder.

No, not a school day. It would probably be a Saturday with its vast stretch of possibility waiting to be claimed in whatever way we wanted. Just enough before jobs and serious homework to let us savor another taste of childhood and just close enough to something beyond childhood to let us know we were not babies anymore.

I'd start my bonus day, after (obviously) a full Iowa home cooked breakfast, by going across the street to see what my grandparents were doing. Grandpa would be sitting in his big over-stuffed chair in front of a window reading a book by holding up a magnifying glass to see the print. He might announce his latest discovery, as when he told me that he'd figured out why black folks were referred to by the N-word. This, he now had it on printed authority was because of a river in Africa named Niger—a discovery which seemed a relief to him in that it explained away the discomfort and guilt the word had previously carried.

Grandma would be close-by working at a little desk-top easel painting in oils. My dad's mother was a widely known local artist. Long ago she had ordered an oil painting kit as a gift for my father at some point in his teen years, and when he failed to be thrilled with the gift, she started playing with it herself. In due course her Adair County farmstead home came to be visited by two big shots from a Chicago art reproduction business—they were trying to recruit my grandma to produce saleable art for their business.

She didn't bite, but eventually she did evolve a small business of her own as neighbors would stop by with photos or with other scenes they'd ripped from a magazine, and ask Grandma to turn into a frame-able oil painting for them. She did, and would be paid sometimes as much as the princely sum (in those days) of twenty dollars for her artistic efforts. She brought her paints and her talent along when she and Grandpa retired and moved into town, and now their living room in Winterset always smelled of oil and turpentine.

Grandma's talent was as a copyist; she could reproduce faithfully any image, in any style, placed in front of her. I sort of understood even then that I should try to get her to produce original art. Why didn't I just take scenic photographs for her, so she could produce art whose inspiration had not been ripped out of a magazine or purloined from a more original artist? I should have. But life is busy when you're an adolescent. Lots of brainstorms were left behind to fend for themselves. Anyway Grandma's work does not hang in any museum but it did back then hang in many homes in Madison and Adair counties.

Everyone seemed to think I must/should have inherited some of her talent, probably because I was an 'artsy' and bookish sort of kid. I did, during my teens, try my hand at drawing and painting because I wanted to be my grandmother's grandson. Somehow the art museums never clamored for my work either, however. Well, it was their loss I have little doubt, although my technique never held a candle to Grandma's.

I never thought of myself as an artsy sort, but I did recognize that I was a bookish sort. And that was already flirting with being uncomfortably different from peer group norms.

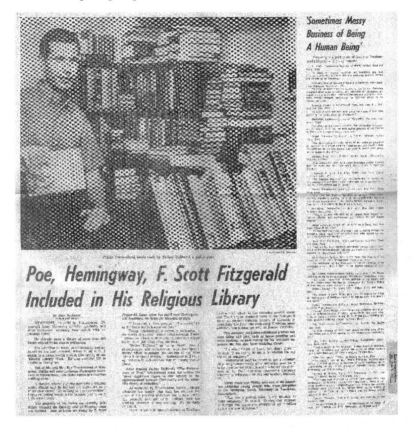

I'd started to cherish and collect books sometime in early high school. When I arrived at the point of needing a place for the growing collection, I asked for an old corner free-standing shelf unit my mother had saved from her own childhood. I sanded it down and re-varnished it, something I could not have conceived of doing in high school shop class where I was supposed to be doing exactly that. I guess my precious books were an adequate motivation, whereas the birds of the air and their need for shelter (I'd spent a semester trying to construct a birdhouse) had not moved me sufficiently to survive 'shop' class with a good grade.

Then the books which I continued to accrue and to love repaid my devotion with the only extra-curricular honor I was to receive at university. The University of Iowa main library asked students to submit catalogues of their personal libraries and mine was named the best of the undergraduate student body at the time. A display of some of my books held sway in the university library for a few weeks, and *The Des Moines Register* ran a long story with a photo of me surrounded by my books and carefully describing some of the more exotic ones.

Of course, the newspaper story encouraged several scolds to write letters suggesting that I didn't read books, but only collected them. Maybe they were trying to assuage their own guilt by passing it on to me. Whatever. I still had the comfort of the expanding worlds to which my books admitted me, and on top of that a little personal celebrity at a still relatively tender age.

As I type this my eyes can't avoid convicting me yet again. My study is filled with great stacks of books all over the floor which have no other resting place. So is the hallway to my bath. Ditto for the entire attic. The first floor is loaded up with hundreds of titles too, but at least we had several walls of bookcases built there before we moved in, as well as a den full of shelves which used to hold the law library of the retired state supreme court justice from whose widow we bought the house—so the first floor scene is at least organized.

By now I might be vulnerable to some extent to the criticism leveled at me by the newspaper readers of my youth. I have not read every book in the house. I have certainly read all of the books looking for a place to roost on the second and third floors. Those on the first floor, however, all books about art and artists, usually painters or sculptors, I have at least read "in." They were to be my retirement project, so technically I should be working on them now. Instead they provide an emotional buffer against each deep New England winter; there will always be something worthwhile to read despite being snowbound (or pandemic bound).

Then on my bonus day I think I'd head to the Square and just walk slowly around it again, slowly enough to enjoy every window display with their suggestions of urbanity and hints at a life which might reach beyond the limitations I was just beginning to suspect constrained us in Winterset. I'd pause outside the bakery to breathe in the sugary fragrance of baking pies and doughnuts. Eventually I'd stop into J.C. Penney's and the Ben Franklin Five and Dime store, siting snuggly next to each other on the south side of the Square, both of which would employ me in years to follow, after school and on weekends, or later still on summer breaks from college. I'd hopefully take special note of the J.C. Penny windows, anticipating the heady days when I got to decorate them myself during high school.

I'd pass the Iowa Theater on the east side of the square and look at the black and white still photos from the current movie offering, and being careful not to trip over the big metal film canisters of the previous feature, now left casually, and safely (this was Winterset, after all) on the sidewalk awaiting pick up.

I'd turn at the corner, just one storefront from the movie theater, and walk past Uncle Scotty's barber shop. There in his window would be a selection of plaster figurines I'd made from rubber molds and hand painted, and had convinced Uncle Scotty to offer for sale to his all-male fresh in from the farm customers—none did ever sell for some odd reason.

I'd walk on toward the Methodist church, the biggest church building in town and just a block from my house. I would have no idea that later, in high school, the church would figure in my lost opportunity for athletic glory and recognition. My high school sports history was essentially nonexistent, although I did go out for basketball in my sophomore year, a career which lasted exactly two practice sessions before I hoisted the white flag of surrender. Later, golf was introduced as a sport and I decided to try again. This was much more successful, probably because the score only reflected self-competition and there were no audiences. But golf never seemed like a sport; it just felt like walking around in a park with a couple of friends.

I'm not even sure why I was aware that near the end of each school year an "all-sports banquet" was held at the Methodist church. But late in my senior year the high school principal, Mr. Miller, approached me in the hallway and asked why I had not attended the sports banquet. "We had a chair reserved for you last night," he announced. For me! You've got to be kidding. At the *sports* banquet? Evidently golf was considered as much a sport as football or basketball, and I had missed my one and only chance to be hailed and fêted as a high school athlete.

Next on this bonus day I'd walk back home to get my trusty bike, maybe stopping on the way into my dad's machine shop just to see what might be happening.

I wasn't much of a chip off the old block, at least in the machine and welding sense of things—that would be left to my brother who went to school in Minneapolis to learn whatever our father couldn't teach him about welding, or whatever he didn't want to learn because the teacher was Dad.

## Leap Year

But I did sense even as a kid that the machine shop was a pretty impressive business capable of fabricating or repairing almost anything in metal needed by the town or its surrounding countryside. This included once a podium lined with bullet-proof steel ordered by the Secret Service to protect President Ronald Reagan when he spoke on the Winterset courthouse steps of the town Square.

*Truckenbrod Machine Shop with Madison County Courthouse in left background*

The shop was a one story brick building with steel rafters one block west of our house and one block east of the Square. It was fairly large and had two big sets of overhead doors to allow entry of the farm implements whose repair was stock-in-trade, or big trucks as the need arose. Inside were all kinds of machines for bending, shaping, grinding, drilling, welding and otherwise manipulating metal. The walls were lined with great racks of steel rods, pipes, and steel sheets waiting their turn to star in some kind of production.

In one corner was a pedestrian entrance and a little office where my mother kept the books and did whatever other paper activities were required of a small business. In the diagonally opposite corner was the realm of the blacksmith with his glowing forge and the anvil upon which he kept up a steady rhythm of clanging beats. Dad's shop even had a mini (miniscule) food court—two coin-operated vending bubbles offering either gumballs or hands-full of peanuts.

Although Dad had built an office room for my mother into the shop near the pedestrian door, her work was never confined to it. After dinner, the table in our kitchen, and often enough the dining room table as well, was usually covered in paper as my mother hand wrote account statements from the work log book.

These then had to be inserted into hand addressed envelopes and stamped. I always marveled that so much handwriting could be accomplished while remaining neat and legible, thinking that my own hand would surely be cramped by that point. Mom was trained in the Palmer Method however, popular in the day, and was a pretty good advertisement for it. She had attended a few semesters at Iowa Teachers College (now the University of Northern Iowa) and had been prepared to teach legible writing to farm kids in a stereotypical one room country school, which she had done for a time before marriage.

These long sessions of writing out statements always furthered my awareness of the current economy because I could overhear my parents discussing their various clients. Some of the accounts had been languishing for many months, or even many growing seasons. We were nearing the end of the heyday of small family farms, and the going was already getting very difficult for them. There was always an undercurrent of angst about long overdue accounts, and whether it was even worth the postage to send yet another statement in some cases. Even so, these same farmers always had a cooperative hand when they needed it at Dad's machine shop. It was simply beyond anyone's imagination to consider cutting off a farmer who needed work done on his equipment, even as his unpaid bills piled up. We were simply all in this together, trying to eke a living out of the rolling prairie.

In an odd way, this machine shop building was one of the town's centers of gravity. Whenever a tractor pulling some kind of plow or harrow or other farm implement could be spotted on a town street, it was a safe bet it was headed to my dad's machine shop.

Beyond repairing farm equipment, the main business activity gradually became the making and installation of wrought iron railings for both residential and commercial sites. Eventually the whole town seemed to be filled with my dad's designs and handiwork. While I wasn't much help in the welding and fabrication aspect of this work, I was evidently capable of being of some assistance in the installation of these railings.

So, often on Saturdays I found myself working beside my dad, like the day he installed a custom order at the biggest of Winterset's funeral homes—memorable not so much because of the lovely hand-crafted railings we were installing, but because of the idle chatter of funeral home workers regaling each other about a client so corpulent that they couldn't locate a large enough coffin. Ha, ha, a real knee slapper.

As I grasped these same railings years later on the way in to my dad's wake, the memories flooded back. Our roots ran so deep in this little town. My parents had labored diligently and left their stamp on the town, but its stamp on us was more profound, and it would never let go.

The only other way my dad found me useful for his business was as a floor sweeper on Saturday mornings, a job which I really detested even though he paid me some pocket money for the effort. It was surprisingly hard work because the metal shavings and tiny metal scraps created a lot of resistance to pushing the big brooms—and because my dad always took a rather no-nonsense approach about expectations. Sometimes my friend Keith would share this work, just as we shared our lawn mowing business, and when my dad turned his back we would grumble to each other that we didn't understand why the machine shop floors had to be "clean enough to eat off of." Evidently my father's Germanic perspective had not successfully transferred to me in an undiluted form.

On one side of the machine shop was an empty corner lot which my grandpa had rented out to the local dealer in new farm implements, and which the dealer used simply for parking his stock. My brother and I routinely cut through this lot diagonally when going up to the Square or returning from it.

One evening after dark I was walking back from my shift at whichever store I was working in at the time, and without thinking cut into the lot. Suddenly a light flooded the scene and a voice called out for me to halt; I'd failed to notice the police car on the street drifting along my route at about my walking pace.

I turned and went over to the cop and started to explain: "I'm Phillip Truckenbrod and...." "Okay, thanks," said the cop, cutting off my explanation and beginning to drive away. Where else but a small town like Winterset would the authorities know all the kids by name and trust them based on the roles their parents played on the civic scene? Later in life I'd live in New York and other large cities and it would become obvious how utterly different life was there for adolescents. We Winterset kids were blessed in ways we simply could not appreciate at the time.

So I would stop by my dad's machine shop on this bonus day and then I'd go down the alley to retrieve my bicycle from our back yard.

Once on wheels I'd certainly want to at least ride past our little brick church, the focus of so much of my life in Winterset. It would still *be* a church on this bonus day. In real life it is no longer that, having been converted to a residence and Bed & Breakfast when, after my time in

Winterset, the congregation relocated to the edge of town for the sake of convenient parking spaces. Even Winterset was not escaping the suburbia craze, to the sacrifice of a way of life where any reasonably healthy person could walk easily and quickly wherever he wanted to go in town. The automobile would come to rule in Winterset, just as it would in the rest of the country.

There is no doubt that my next destination would be my friend Doug's house, the lovely big Victorian home where I'd spent my childhood when not in school or church or at my parents' house. And Doug would still be there, or at least still live there and not near Des Moines where he moved in the middle of high school, to my sadness.

If Doug were not at home just then, I could ride on almost anywhere in town reliving happy times. Traffic would never be much of a problem; a bike rider had to be only minimally alert to avoid danger. And the well-kept homes of the West end of town provided a calm setting for casual sightseeing; although not so much for people-watching. To see people on the street one really did need to go to the Square. So this souvenir bike ride really wouldn't require a very specific focus—it would be enough just to be enveloped by Winterset again; to relive another few hours in the safety and uncomplicated pleasure of her always welcoming, and usually forgiving, embrace.

## CUSP OF A NEW ERA

The Winterset I knew is mostly gone now no matter how much the Square looks about the same as it always did. Even the prairie gods cannot actually 'turn back the hands of time.' They can only let me visit my Winterset through the haze of imperfect memory. A new modern and technological era has emerged that was only hinted at vaguely at the cusp of its predecessor period in the middle of last century.

Kids today have to coach their parents in how to run the ubiquitous electronic devices which dominate our lives. In my day it was the reverse; parents still had to help their children cope with the faint beginnings of this new age. Take just the hard wired telephone—now almost forgotten even by adults and encountered by their kids only as museum pieces.

My own first encounter with a telephone came in my grandma's farm kitchen. There, amidst objects like hand-worked churns for turning whole milk into the delights of butter and buttermilk, objects which exist today only in museums, another object hung on the wall about the size of an extra-large shoe box.

It had a crank which one turned a few times to activate the genie who lived inside. Then one took a black thing off a hook on the side of the box, and connected to it by a cord, and held one end of it to one's ear while speaking into another weird looking object projecting from the front of the box. Then one told the genie who you wanted to reach verbally, "Connect me with the Jones farm please—no, Sam Jones, not Bill." As the Jones phone was being connected, one would hear several clicks on the line, and when the conversation concluded, several more clicks could be heard, and one's neighbors from miles around knew exactly what you had to tell Sam, and what he told you in reply.

Party line telephones were not only the forerunners of hand-held cell phones, they were also the forerunners of the entertainment features on cell phones. My grandma taught me when and how to pick up the ear piece just at the right time to listen in on her neighbors' chatter.

In town, telephones only gradually made their appearances in private homes; the early ones showed up mostly in businesses. There were differences from my grandparents' phone in appearance and convention: "Connect me with 4545, please," one told the genie, although if you had forgotten the digits you could still throw yourself on the genie's mercy, "I'm trying to reach Bob Smith on Elm Street but I don't know the number, sorry." One of the genies would show you a little kindness by taking a plug attached to a heavy chord and plugging it into a particular hole on a big board with lots of different holes. Then some neighbors might contribute their little clicks just like the farm folks did and the community could rally around the latest news.

The telephone genies lived in a house just behind our public library. Eventually they figured out how to keep the neighbors from participating in our phone calls, thus propelling us further into the new era or killing another innocent joy, depending upon one's point of view. Still further along the way the genies figured out how to stop listening to us order them around.

Telephones grew appendages of little wheels with several holes through which one could see an assortment of numbers and letters. One just stuck one's finger in a hole and twisted the wheel and then let it spring back to its original position. Then repeat three, eventually seven times with different finger holes and suddenly, like magic, one could hear the telephone ringing no matter how far away lived the person one was calling. The telephone genies were surely pushing us toward a new age, but I'm not convinced they ever stopped listening in on our calls.

The first "modern" telephone in my life was located in my dad's machine shop business. If one of my parents needed to reach someone urgently, they walked up the alley to the shop. In due course I guess they felt they were financially secure enough to place one of these newfangled devices in their house as well.

On the otherwise routine evening of the day our house phone was installed they walked up the alley to check whether all the shop machines had been properly turned off for the day, a habit my father had firmly established with religious inflexibility. I was at home and I heard, for the first time, our new telephone ring. I panicked. I knew something important was happening but I had no idea what I was supposed to do about it. So I ran out of the house and up the alley towards the machine shop to tell my parents that there was an emergency and they had to rush home to answer the telephone. Half way there I encountered them returning—and they laughed at my urgent pleas to rush home. They had been trying to prank me by sending the first telephone call into our house when I was the only one who could cope with it.

Eventually I did learn how (or gathered the courage) to answer a telephone, but now it's a lost art unless one counts talking into those little flat things everyone carries around in their pockets; those things which started life as huge black boxes we saw Londoners carrying around long before they were to be found here; those little things which no longer have just a genie living inside them, but an entire computer. And, by the way, we now seem to know the genie's name; she's "Siri" and she's listening all the time. Just say anything which sounds vaguely like her name and she springs into action, ready to help, or to make a sarcastic comment if you reply in a way she considers rude. ⌘

# 21 Every Season of the Year
## Be Nice

"There's nothing half-way about the Iowa way we greet you, if we greet you, which we may not do at all," Meredith Wilson's *The Music Man* chorus sang.

He certainly had it at least half right, the part about maybe not doing it at all being just a bit of theatrical drama because Iowans *will* greet you, whether you want to be greeted or not (although the later lyrics about "Iowa Stubborn" could ring true).

Iowans are just plain nice. It's part of their identity, maybe part of their DNA. It's also a strongly felt obligation. If an Iowan has something disapproving to say about you, it's a safe bet he will not say it to your face, and he may just swallow it down completely and not say it even to his spouse. On the street, in the store, in public anywhere, all is tranquil, courteous, and civil. Is this hypocritical? No, it's just Iowa. If we can't always agree, let's at least keep our civil discourse civil.

If an Iowan disagrees with you, the only hint I can suggest for knowing so is that the Iowan may be silent on the subject in question. He's certainly not going to make a public spectacle of disagreement because that might hurt your feelings. Better for him just to remain silent.

If I ask an old friend from Iowa for a favor, or for advice or information, and hear nothing in return, then I know I have my answer—he certainly is not going to actually refuse in so many words; if he must refuse for whatever reason, he will do so by remaining silent. If there is subsequent contact, my original request or question just never happened. If there is any rule all Iowans follow strictly, it's "if you can't say anything nice about someone, don't say anything at all." Actually, I think that's the state motto, despite some other words written on our flag.

Certainly if you want to understand Iowa, you need to master niceness. To fit in, you may have to train yourself to be nicer than nature has equipped you to be on your own. Iowa nice is not necessarily easy; it may not come naturally to some people. Iowa nice is tough, rugged, deliberate, organized, systematic—and even at times aggressive. Iowa nice is not an accident. It's a decision, a choice of life-style. It's a tribal characteristic which can't be violated without loss of status, or even membership, in the tribe. Iowans are simply determined to be nice.

The result is pleasant. Maybe a bit lacking in suspense, but pleasant. Iowa nice is something like our landscape. Our hills are pleasantly rolling prairie hills, never jagged or too steep, just smoothly rolling enough to be interesting but never startling.

So too are our public personalities. One is surrounded by non-judgmental (at least to one's face) fellow citizens. It is therefore safe to err upon occasion because one knows one will not be called on the error, at least not in public and not with malice. If there is any stated objection to the error, it will be delivered more in sorrow than in triumph, and probably with an apology regardless of who was actually right in the matter.

Such an atmosphere can be liberating in that one feels able to test a dubious idea out loud (upon occasion; but don't make a habit of it) because probably no one within ear-shot is going to jump down your throat. If they disagree, they would probably simply remain silent on the subject. If they say anything in response it would be gentle, and designed more to help educate the offender than to punish him—and certainly not designed to embarrass him.

This behavior was a social covenant. One did not depart from the code because one did not want one's neighbors to depart from it either. We lived the Golden Rule by being so nice to each other. No wonder it felt a little like a religious obligation. We had evolved to value the placid in our relationships. Iowa niceness was not an invention of the Chamber of Commerce; it had become organic in our lives.

Even so, being nice to each other is not exactly a widely observed human trait on the world stage. It didn't always come naturally or easily in every human contact, even in Iowa. So we kept on *deciding* to be nice; it was a trait which had to be practiced if one were to stay in shape, like an athlete keeping his muscles limber. We were just relentlessly nice. Did we really believe in all this pleasantness? Yes, I think so, because we wanted to, and because we needed to. We wanted to live in a nice place, and therefore we had to keep creating the Iowa we wanted to live in.

At the same time, however, all this pleasantness could also be a bit binding and restrictive. This was the case because the Iowa code did not permit one to say anything which one knew in advance might offend or overtly challenge the hearer. That's probably why I can't remember politics ever being discussed at family dinners, even though we did have a black sheep uncle whose views were always contrary to the prevailing norm.

When I ponder the roots of all of this niceness, I think it might be a direct consequence of early life on the prairie. Life for those European settlers was hard, even brutal on the open swaths of Midwestern grasslands. Nature provided sufficient challenge. There was no need to complicate life at home, or relationships with neighbors, by introducing social friction as well. So 'Iowa Nice' may have evolved as a form of self-preservation, or at least as an emotional balancing mechanism—the social equivalent of a cozy warm hearth to fend off the cold and the threatening.

Our Midwestern neighbors can be rather nice too, and Minnesota is guilty of the theft of claiming to be "Minnesota Nice." I've even heard people from Wisconsin being referred to as "nice." Most likely our neighbors are nice because of our Iowa good example; our niceness has just rubbed off onto them across the border.

But it's Iowans who are really, truly, inescapably and incorrigibly NICE. Only a few years ago a video production company in the state made a fairly long run of "Iowa Nice" features, many of which ran on national television. These productions also yielded regular interviews on the sports networks with the "Mr. Iowa Nice Guy" who was asked to pontificate (nicely, of course) on the football prospects of various college teams, and especially those of Iowa and Iowa State.

During my first two years of college, at Wartburg in Waverly, someone once forgot to greet a passing fellow student rushing between classes. If you're not an Iowan that might seem to be the smallest of possible infractions, but the offended (ignored) student was incensed. The insult became a matter of heated campus discussion for weeks, finally ending up on the agenda of the student senate (although I was a senate member at the time, I don't remember just how the senate planned to enforce niceness as a policy).

It became clear after much falderal that any student crossing the path of another student was absolutely expected, nay required, to offer at least a quick "hello," even if it was not the first time these particular students had crossed paths that day. We were in Iowa, after all—we should be nice to each other.

There must have been almost a threat of exhaustion from needing to say "Hello" so many times in a day, and frequently to the same person. Now I look back and wonder if we actually said "Hello" to each other when we encountered another naked person in the dorm gang shower. (This sentence began as a kind of gratuitous smart-aleck remark, but the more I think back the more convinced I have become that, indeed, we did greet each other in the showers just as heartily and without fail as we did outside on campus pathways.)

If you visit Iowa and stop to eat in a restaurant or diner, in the city or out in the countryside, expect to be greeted like a long-lost relative. Your server is not just hoping for a bigger tip; s/he is being an Iowan and giving you your due as a visitor to Iowa.

As a young adult on quick visits home from my new perch in the more aloof confines of the East Coast, I was often disconcerted by such Iowa friendliness. People would greet me on the street with such enthusiasm and apparently heart-felt energy that I'd go off thinking "who the xxxx was that?" Did he actually remember me? Did he know my name even though I could no longer remember his, assuming I ever knew it at all? Or was I a complete stranger, and he was just being Iowa Nice? There seemed no way to tell the difference.

I once complained about this to my mother and suggested such greetings could have a hypocritical ring to them. "Oh, they're just trying to be nice," she answered, a little bewildered that I should have objected to someone being so nice to me. That's the way the world is in Iowa—Nice. Officially nice. I've never completely figured out whether I miss all that niceness now, or if I'm happier in the urban East where people try to avoid eye-contact so they don't have to bother being nice at all.

I guess I can say that my Iowa training in being nice no longer feels like a burden. It may even at times feel like an advantage. Maybe to throw a sop at honesty, I should admit that Iowans were not always especially nice to absolutely everyone. Niceness was not so much a human right as a tribal right; a tribal characteristic and a tribal privilege, and often a requirement only inside the tribe. It was sometimes reserved for 'our kind,' *aka* 'people like us.'

But the borders which defined 'people like us' were generally located at the edge of town. "Those people" lived in Des Moines or some other place primarily defined by not being Winterset. Being Iowans we recognized that we probably owed them perfunctory niceness to their faces, but not necessarily niceness when we talked about them after getting back to the safe confines of our cocoons.

Yes, if one searched hard enough one could uncover little exceptions to the "Iowa Nice" rule. Still, the important part was that we realized that we *should* be nice, and therefore that we actually *tried* to be nice for the most part. It's the thought that matters, to phrase it in still more of Iowa's argot.

## ONE THREATENING GRAY CLOUD ON THE HORIZON

All of this niceness and goodwill made for a very comfortable place to live. However, a lot of us, I suspect, did not want to push the envelope too far—we weren't exactly sure where the niceness might suddenly run into a wall of Winterset limestone. I, perhaps like a lot of others, was by high school beginning to be vaguely aware that there were aspects of my being which didn't fit snuggly into the cozy outline prescribed for us; a little something which might not be perceived as being as 'nice' as we were all trying to be.

So, about the little matter of my not especially robust attraction to girls.

That, thankfully, managed not to acquire a name until the first semester of grad school by which time I'd already enjoyed twenty-two years of relatively untortured innocence. Without a name it was, at worst, a nagging suspicion that usually could be brushed aside fairly easily for another long period of blissful ignorance. And Winterset for me *was* a period of innocence. I'm grateful Winterset was never put to the test of knowing the name of my uncomfortable secret; the one I kept squelching back and for the most part ignoring. While I'd like to believe Winterset would have continued her militantly "Iowa Nice" posture, and kept me hugged close as a son of the town, there's no way to be absolutely sure.

We were growing up, and among the many things that meant was that while we could still hide some things from our parents, and even from our peers, we were losing the ability to hide things from ourselves.

My first general media hint that something dark, threatening, and extremely intriguing was 'out there' came in high school senior year in a grand old movie theater in Des Moines. Why I chose to see "Suddenly, Last Summer" (and to see it alone, not with my usual two 'double-dating' movie partners) I know not exactly, although promotion of the film must have vaguely hinted at things I felt I should know about. Nor could I quite figure out just then, sitting in a big old fashioned movie palace by myself in the city, why on the screen Sebastian Venable kept attracting boys on the beach, and *certainly* not why these boys eventually attacked him *en masse*.

I left the big movie palace confused. But I did know instantly that all of this strange and odd stuff did somehow apply to me. I was somehow involved in this, and it felt not only weird but threatening. Something I didn't understand and couldn't name had a very powerful hold over me, and I was gradually losing the ability to keep it at arm's length; to keep kicking that particular can down the road.

The periods of regressing back into blissful ignorance were becoming fewer and more difficult to extend. Was I the only kid in my class, or even in the whole Winterset school system at the time, to be in the throes of this torture? Statistically that seems unlikely. But statistics and averages are not necessarily spread out evenly. And furthermore, the ethos of the time dictated that such matters were not to be articulated then back in the 1950's, so there could have been dozens of us struggling in our own dark little caves without the comfort of company, or even of knowing for sure that we weren't the only humans in the entire world blessed with this curse.

I am glad that Winterset was not put to the test on this score. It was certainly better, as I was beginning to understand intuitively, to live out the last few months and weeks of my allotted time there still able to hold tightly to some degree of childhood innocence. College and university were ahead, and more school after that before I had to accept and cope with the imperfections of adulthood. Whatever the fears of our shortcomings, we just had to hold on a bit longer to emerge from our Winterset school days relatively unscathed. Winterset was our age of innocence and it should remain so as an anchor to help us weather the coming storms of adult reality.

So among the many cherished friends of childhood and adolescence I have not the faintest idea if any shared with me the peculiarity which came to shape my life in a way I had never expected. But Winterset had done its job. It had given me a firm foundation of niceness and self-confidence upon which to launch myself into the sometimes icy winds of what some were beginning to call the "real world." ⌘

# 22 A Town For All Seasons

Winterset on a map is fairly typical of Iowa county seat towns.

At its center is a square (or, the Square if one is not speaking geometrically) upon which sits the county courthouse. Around this Square is the commercial heart of the town, with a full block of retail business buildings facing the courthouse from each cardinal direction.

These commercial buildings were (and still are) only two stories in height, but two very high stories, so that the over-all impression was of perhaps three story buildings. Residential apartments occupied most of these second floors. The facades were generally of red brick with architectural decorations in molded concrete or, more likely carved into stone, and gave a vaguely Victorian impression. They were handsome buildings which blended their facades harmoniously along the sides of the trees and great tower of the courthouse Square—it never crossed my mind that we were anything other than blessed to live in such a place.

Off of this grid the next blocks radiating from the corners of the square were also about a block's length-full of assorted other business, or public institutions such as the library and 'City' Hall.

These businesses on the radiating streets tended to be less retail and more agriculturally oriented (farm supplies, a chicken hatchery), plus doctors' clinics, and auto dealerships, etc. Thus there were a nice even dozen facing commercial blocks forming the heart of town, the Square. Most people seemed to think it was all very picturesque and tidy and I agreed with them.

My time on the Square was mostly spent in three of the establishments that gave me employment during my Winterset school years. But one of the radiating blocks also supplied a relatively brief period of employment after my grandmother recommended me to our family doctor. He had need of an inexpensive person to do a weekly general clean up and floor mopping at his office just across the street from the public library.

Actually, that particular radiating block was a fairly substantial part of my school days. The library provided many happy days of discovery.

Directly across the street, however, the enthusiasm level dropped off sharply. There, neatly side-by-side in a little row of potential anxiety, were located some of a school boy's favorite store fronts: our family doctor, our dentist, and our optometrist. I seem to have survived them all; or maybe it was they who helped me to survive beyond Winterset.

The first thing which made Winterset stand out a bit from the crowd of 99 Iowa county seat towns was the Madison County courthouse itself.

This classically styled building was in cruciform shape with four identical porticos facing the commercial sides of the Square, and sporting fairly massive columns made of native (Madison County) limestone, as was the entire structure below the central tower.

In the center was, and is to this day, a large and (compared to any nearby buildings) very tall round tower. In my day this massive tower was a stately silver but somewhere along the line it was painted in a perhaps misguided redecoration. This tower could be seen looming above the tree line from almost any direction one approached town. If you were a total stranger, you might even have guessed from a distance that you were approaching the state's capital city, so large, dramatic and elegant was the silver tower.

Or at least I used to conjure that image as a kid walking back into town from a hike and seeing the first glimpse of the courthouse tower and the Iowa state flag flying proudly over the highway department garage at Winterset's edge.

During my early years as a Wintersetonian (?) this tower was actually flat on top, although it came to such a graceful culmination no one thought of it that way. At some point the town fathers decided it needed a lantern on top, and hired a local welding shop to construct and install one. I've always questioned its simplistic design as not really doing justice to rest of the building (it always reminds me of a Chinese double-gourd ceramic on top of a Greek temple), but it is undeniable that this lantern finished off the tower nicely and added more drama as one approached town. It gave us an enhanced "skyline."

The installation of this lantern was a great spectacle and folks watched from their porches or yards, especially as the night work lights added to the impression of seeing a skyscraper rise.

For me, however, fascinated as I was, watching was a guilty pleasure.

The guy who made and was installing the lantern was a former business partner of my father. They had started business in town with a machine shop bearing both their sur-names. When they split, the other partner had opened a rival machine shop to Dad's and our family suddenly had local business competitors. Although a child, I knew that there were sore feelings still afoot.

So when I watched the rising lantern in awe from my grandfather's front lawn, I did so with a guilt which made me feel a bit traitorous and sneaky. My parents said very little about this great civic event, at least within my hearing. (As it turned out, my dad's former business partner evidently couldn't make a go of running his own machine shop and before too long was off on a completely unrelated tangent, despite leaving behind his vivid mark on the town Square.)

The other aspect which made Winterset stand out was a collection of old covered bridges scattered in its nearby countryside. They were all painted barn-red and looked like refuges from New England.

In my day there were seven of these bridges. One has since been lost to intentional vandalism (arson), and another has been moved into our city park where it's available to more eyes and where it's easier to keep an eye *on* it. After my Winterset years these bridges have become more widely famous because of Robert James Waller's best-selling novel "The Bridges of Madison County" and then especially so from the movie version of the same name.

On subsequent visits home I've seen plenty of tourists pull off the highway to take photographs of the signs pointing out the side road to one or another of these bridges—presumably these folks made it as far as the actual bridge to take more photos. The local Chamber of Commerce, upon which there are no flies, found its own way to capitalize by organizing "Covered Bridge Days," a festival which annually brings to town lots of visitors, and not just city people from Des Moines looking for an easy day-trip, but genuinely foreign tourists from several continents.

When I was growing up in Winterset, we were aware of two celebrities who had graced our little town. George Washington Carver had lived there for a time (why so I don't remember being told) and there was a marker next to the fire station to remind the world of that.

And Marion Mitchell Morrison had been born in Winterset. Despite many a Saturday afternoon watching John Wayne movies in the small Iowa Theater on the town Square, I always felt that the biggest honor our town gleaned from these two celebrities came from George. However, as in so many areas of life, I didn't speak for the majority. They voted overwhelmingly for John (or Marion).

Now our main street, which used to be plain old State Highway 92, or 'First Street,' is called "John Wayne Drive," and visitors come from all over the world (I'm given to believe) to see the small white frame house where (gasp), JOHN WAYNE (!) was born.

I've only seen the outside of the newish John Wayne Museum, vacillating as I do between pride that Winterset now has a museum of any variety, and mild embarrassment that it has to be for a movie actor. In the middle of writing this book, John (my John, not John Wayne) and I made a little pilgrimage back to Winterset just to refresh memories. We drove past the John Wayne birthplace and museum, and found them buzzing with tourists. After pulling over briefly to admire (?) the nearly life-sized bronze statue of the actor which stands in the museum's front courtyard, we drove on, unable to stir up enough interest to make it worth our while to actually go inside.

When we had lunch a few minutes later on the Winterset Square with my sister-in-law and my great niece they both admitted never having entered the museum either, out of sheer lack of interest.

Yeah, I'm perhaps being a bit of a snob. But most of the good folks of Winterset are not; they're proud as punch flavored pop to claim John Wayne in as many ways as possible. Or could it simply be that they have a well developed sense of practicality and the ability to take advantage of whatever scraps circumstances throw their way?

John Wayne, however, apparently did not return the enthusiasm. Leaving Winterset when his parents moved to California, he never returned—not for one of the many events held to honor him, and not for the dedication of any of the several sites in town built or preserved to honor him. Local boy makes good? Skip the 'local boy' part.

But, hey. We could live with that and still 'make hay' (Iowa, you know) anyway. Being overlooked and under-valued never stopped us before. This was Iowa before the presidential caucuses were discovered by Jimmy Carter, and we were used to making the best of living in fly-over country. So ignore the insult, and make hay from John Wayne whether he cares or not—after all, no one asked him to be born in Winterset so he's fair game. And besides that, the presidential caucuses probably died in 2020 so we now need John Wayne even more than before.

## A BOYHOOD PARADISE

Winterset made a perfect place for a curious and healthy boy of the mid-twentieth century to grow up. It was large enough to reflect life in catholic dimensions, although there may have been only one of everything, and sometimes maybe only a hint of some other aspects of life or commerce. And yet it was small enough to own and comprehend. It was a satisfactory little universe for a grade school boy who lived in town and had his own wheels; in those days a bicycle was almost indistinguishable from the kid who owned it. Roller boards and scooters were still a bit in the future, although we did have roller skates of course, but they were mostly for going around one's own block (or by the high school years for dating at commercial rinks in Des Moines), whereas bicycles offered what seemed to be limitless travel possibilities.

With bicycles we explored not only our town, but the countryside surrounding it and other, tiny, hamlets which were sprinkled about in Madison County. Peru was a favorite, perhaps because it sounded funny as a name. And then there was the iconic Podunk which was so famous in the abstract as a symbol of small town America that we felt it must really amount to something despite its miniscule size; actually, I think it was so small as to be nothing more than an intersection, a gas station, and a name—but one of several such named hamlets in many states and thus legendary.

And none of this required any disobedience or sneaking around. Parents were happy to grant us these freedoms. They never stopped to worry about our safety, except perhaps for an occasional skinned knee. Predators, human ones, of whatever stripe, didn't seem to have been invented yet. Quite the opposite actually. If a kid needed help while out of the house, everyone felt safe to assume that the first adult encountered would rush to give assistance. This was an "it takes a village" age and setting in the very best sense.

How many times I may have been a beneficiary of this village parenting I can't be sure, but I do vividly remember one example, probably because it embarrassed me.

I had set out by bicycle to get something at a neighborhood grocery store, and suddenly could not recall which street it was on, and thus at which intersection I was supposed to turn left. I rode right into the intersection absorbed with this problem and looking intently to my left for a clue. Suddenly I came back into the moment and found myself and my bike just inches ahead of a stopped car in the middle of the street. The driver wore an understanding and gentile smile on his face, as if remembering his own boyhood foibles. He had stopped for me even though it should have been my job to stop for him. He didn't yell at me although he probably should have. He hadn't honked the car horn before I rode in front of his car, although maybe he should have. He didn't reproach me in any way although I deserved to be lectured. He just accepted the situation with bemusement, and had accepted all of the responsibility for a good outcome on his own shoulders. He had assumed the parental role, as the unwritten code of our small town required.

In addition to bicycling anywhere we wanted, Winterset was small enough to walk anywhere in town (yet large enough to have places worth walking to). I must have walked past M. Young and Company thousands of times as a school boy; it was on my route to church, the post office, the library, to my friend Doug's house—a landmark and fixture in my childhood. M. Young was a grain elevator and feed/seed store which, aside from the courthouse, was Winterset's only "skyscraper," or so it seemed to me. It was located a block north of the Square and whenever I passed it the odors of our agricultural surroundings would please the nose; grain, straw, corn. It was to M. Young we'd go as kids to buy feed for pet rabbits or pet chickens, or for me, pet pigeons also.

By the time Hollywood rediscovered Winterset (there had been at least one movie shot there earlier) and used it as the set for filming "The Bridges of Madison County," M. Young had been closed but the buildings still made their contribution to our skyline. The movie folks saw value in this abandoned business, but not on its own terms, although it could easily have figured in the plot on its own terms. They installed a country general store of their own imagining at M. Young and used it in a key movie scene. I don't think Winterset ever actually had a general store of that sort, but the movie set seemed to agree with what 'outsiders' expected of a small Iowa town.

The filming of that movie, obviously a local sensational event, probably touched a lot of Winterset families in a variety of ways. My family's involvement, and contribution, came through my brother who was the chief of the town's volunteer fire department for a couple of decades. The movie producers needed a driving rain to establish the mood of the scene, but filmed it on a bright sunny day. My brother's fire equipment and colleagues were called into service to train their hoses on the 'action' and provide the scripted deluge.

Just behind M. Young & Co. stood our little railroad depot, painted red and looking as stereotypically American Midwest as you could possibly want. This train depot always fascinated me. I dreamt of the long gone days when passenger trains could whisk one off to far away places right from our own doorsteps.

We still had trains going through town, but they were there to carry material from the rock and gravel quarries (Winterset was built on a large deposit of limestone) near town into Des Moines for processing and further distribution. Our passenger service, when we had it, was probably just a car or two added to the gravel trains, but I reveled in imagining those more cosmopolitan times for our little town. One nice thing the rock trains still did have, though, was a caboose at the end; an appealing throw-back in time but which seemed to have no identifiable current purpose.

## A Town for All Seasons

These remaining daily trains were the bane of my dad, however. Our house was built right next to the rail right-of-way and the trains operated without the faintest hint of an established schedule. Day or night, early or late, the trains just rode past whenever they wanted. My father seemed to lay awake at night fearing that one would come past to wake him up!

The trains had not carried passengers for as long as anyone seemed to remember. For the few folks left in town who lacked an automobile, the only public transportation still available was the daily Greyhound bus. A number of folks still used the bus to get back and forth from Des Moines, probably mostly for routine shopping. The bus station in Winterset was wherever the driver could find to park on a side street near one of the corners of the Square. The ticket counter was the check-out desk at one of the town's little cafes near that corner. The waiting room was standing on your own feet outside, regardless of the weather.

For me the bus was an occasional means to get into Des Moines, usually with my friend Doug and his mother. She would occasionally go in to visit her husband during the working week, leaving Doug and me with a little big city exploration time so long as we did not stray beyond a prescribed perimeter.

For my Aunt Ina and Uncle Scotty, that bus was the gateway to the rest of the world; or at least to the rest of the country. They made a number of trips all the way to California to visit his relatives, and a number all the way to New York to assuage a constant wanderlust, plus a bit of north-south travelling to boot, thus covering the length and width of our great nation. To be able to do that beginning from and returning to the Winterset Square without an automobile seemed pretty cosmopolitan to me. And as a kid I never had reason to doubt that life in Winterset was anything but that.

Although pretty much a carefree kid, I too had some misgivings about those trains my dad resented. I always had pet dogs, and in Winterset dogs were rarely kept inside, so they ran free and the giant trains dieseling past our house posed a danger on the pet front I did occasionally worry about. None of my dogs were ever sacrificed to the monster trains, although occasionally one fell victim to an automobile or to a neighbor's rat poison. Actually I ran over one of my dogs myself. He always ran alongside our bicycles barking at the front wheel. Once he stumbled for some reason and went completely under the wheel. He showed no outward signs of damage as a result and lived well beyond the incident.

Across the street from the little red train depot with its proud "Winterset" sign, was our municipal electricity generating plant. Why at that point we generated our own electricity rather than connecting to a larger grid I'm not sure. But the noise of the plant's three inside diesel generators was a constant Winterset music. I guess some of what I'm writing could make Winterset seem more of a hell than a paradise, but for a school-boy it was everything one could want.

The train tracks did not turn at the station, but went on a couple blocks more to a "turn table" used to swivel the engine around to head in the opposite direction. This amounted to a large bridge-like platform of heavy timbers which rotated to line up with the tracks as needed. The pit beneath this apparatus was always filled with a couple feet of water which hosted creatures of interest to exploring boys. Mostly these were crayfish of some sort, which we called "crawdaddies." One of the town's boy-duties was to catch these creatures, although I'm not sure why we wanted to or what we did with them beyond tossing them back into the water.

I'm disappointed to need to report that the little red train depot is no longer standing proudly at its spot. It was moved away when the tracks were removed, leaving now just an empty plot of grass looking incongruous and wasteful in its setting near the Square. Knowing the Winterset spirit, it's almost baffling to me that evidently no one saw the potential that little red depot held for the town, especially as it grew as a regional tourist destination. It would have made a dandy tourist information center, or souvenir shop, and there was ample room for a parking lot. The train tracks are gone now as well. The only remaining physical evidence of the Winterset trains is a curious empty strip of land running through a large section of town. (The depot itself at least ended up in the little mock village created by the county historical society.)

This area, between the actual tracks and the side street they ran along, an area about twenty feet wide, was opened for adjoining home owners to purchase after the tracks were taken out. No one bit, I gather, mostly for fear of increasing their property taxes. So the town solved its problem by simply deeding sections of the former rail right-of-way to each adjoining property owner, thereby turning the land into taxable property whether the new owners liked that or not. Today it's a parade of grass through the residential neighborhood. The only property owner I could spot to have actually utilized this added land was my nephew, who built a garage on it facing the side street. No one else, in so far as I could see, even bothered to plant a tree on their windfall of added territory.

Winterset had just enough to keep a boy happy. There was the town park close enough in to either bike or walk to at will. And there was Benoit's mini-grocery on the way to stock up on candy or other necessities for the excursion. ('Benoit' was resolutely pronounced 'Ben-noyt' perhaps to dispel any notion that we might have been influenced by the French. Fear of European contamination probably also accounted for my family

## A Town for All Seasons

name always being mispronounced 'Truck-in-broad,' which I hated, as have succeeding generations of my kin living in Winterset.)

One also passed the "monument works" where gravestones were cut and inscribed for the town cemetery, and where I once asked for a granite sample. I was given, in typical small town Iowa generosity to a mere kid, a small rectangle of highly polished Vermont granite which I treasure to this day. Once arrived at the park there were miles of wooded trails and roads to explore, and convenient fireplaces to grill hot dogs and marshmallows; not to mention a variety of playground equipment.

The town park also tipped its hat to local history. A rustic log cabin, valued because it figured in the founding of the town, had long ago been moved to the park and restored. It was in this simple structure that a group of citizens had met in the mid-nineteenth century to charter and name the place, as I mentioned to you early on.

Another monument in the park of school-boy intrigue was a large boulder with attached bronze plaque commemorating an apple tree which had once stood in a corner of a field of corn on a near-by farm. This was the parent tree of all "Delicious" apples, by then popular world-wide and all owing to grafts from the Madison County original tree.

The friendliness (toleration?) local business people had for little boys begging for things was a small town virtue I and my peers took for granted. Once I went through a 'decal' phase after discovering the colorful stickers popular with tourists back then ("This car climbed Mt. Washington," etc.). I decided to make a collection of them. In-town sources could supply only advertising decals related to their businesses (auto dealerships, etc.) but I managed to acquire a fairly large collection. It was surprising how many could be gleaned from a small county-seat town, and how generously the business people would respond to a pesky little boy collecting them. Of course, I was not content to just collect them—I then had to actually apply them. Mostly I glued them onto a large framed mirror in my room which had been passed along by my grandparents—my mother was not overly pleased by this choice of location for my collection.

My brother and I also cherished and constantly played with some business paraphernalia I'd begged off our Greenfield grandfather, twenty miles over in the next county. He ran a gas station and I always loved the strings of colorful pennants such fueling stations usually used to attract attention. Grandpa came up with a long string of these as a gift, along with a metal sign advertising automotive oil.

Richard and I would set up imaginary fairs and stores in the back yard, stringing the rope of pennants between an apple tree and the garage, and dragging out the oil sign for prominent display.

Then we decided to widen our commercial sights. Our other grandpa, across the street in Winterset, was then building wooden easy chairs for outside use. We persuaded him to make us dealers for selling these chairs. So we took our string of red-blue-white pennants to the front yard between trees, and set up a street-side display of grandpa's chairs painted various loud colors. We managed to sell none of them, but then traffic was pretty light on our street, and by the next day we were on to other horizons.

Winterset actually had two large parks. The other was a state park a few miles outside town. It was the scene of many Boy Scout encampments in our later grade school years, and it was very popular locally for its tunnel through a limestone ridge, unique in Iowa, and a river crossing which was a submerged slab of concrete so that one had the illusion of driving over the water.

A bunch of us were bicycling out to the state park one day when I got a very painful surprise which most likely every boy has gotten at some point, although perhaps in other circumstances. Boys and girls bikes were militantly different in those days, and boys' bicycles had a solid bar running from just under the seat to the handle bar support. Girls' bikes, on the other hand, were absent that bar because the drapery of skirts and dresses needed to be accommodated, in theory at least, although girls of our age were allowed to wear more accommodating clothing when riding their bikes.

Going up a little hill while standing on the pedals for greater power, the gear suddenly slipped and I found myself riding on that bar with my feet dangling off the sides. Pain? Excruciating pain! It was my turn to have the "I'll never be able to have children" moment every boy has had at some point or another.

Even the adults could have their problems riding out to the state park. One of the contributions made to our area by all the limestone deposits was an abundance of rattlesnake dens. Snake hunting took its place along side critter hunting for local men, and I can remember seeing some very large rattlesnake specimens displayed in our neighbor's yard after one such hunt. Sometimes the county government even staged official rattlesnake hunts with prizes awarded and records kept for the largest specimens killed.

Anyway, these snakes had a tendency to want to cross our highways. It was not at all unusual to spot them, alive or already having been run over by a car, on the short stretch of highway between town and the state park. The wife of one of the town's prominent businessmen was well known for refusing to drive or ride on that highway, being certain that a rattlesnake would somehow grab onto the car's undercarriage and then drop off again in her driveway back in town. Whether other Winterset matrons shared this phobia I'm not sure, but at least it had a specifically local flavor.

Winterset had neat and clear cut boundaries during my childhood years. On one side of the last street would be a continuation of the grid pattern with decently spaced houses proclaiming "town." On the other side of that street would be a cornfield; simple and non-ambiguous: the countryside starts here.

Could it have been that Winterset was actually longing for a suburban look all those years? Now the boundary between town and cornfield is vague and ill-defined, with houses of recent vintage sprouting up in the cornfields. Churches have abandoned their town buildings to show up anew on the edge of town where ample parking is the current "golden calf" (the little in-town brick church of my childhood is now a Bed and Breakfast). Winterset now has its own "suburbs" in a sense, while at the same time having itself become virtually a suburb of Des Moines (our population has soared into the near stratosphere too, with the constant 3,500 +/- of my day now around 5,250). There are still wide open miles separating Winterset from the state capital, but now everyone (it seems) from Winterset works, shops, plays, eats and drinks in Des Moines, returning home only to sleep a bit before commuting in again.

What for me had been Eden on the prairie seems now to be flirting with becoming a diorama of American small town life, a museum of how Iowans used to live.

## WINTERSET THE SECURE

All of the Iowa niceness I've already explained to you was a factor which affected our lives in practical ways too, not just in emotional ways. Perhaps because we expected everyone to be so nice, we convinced ourselves that no one would (could?) actually be un-nice.

Back then locks were an ignored possibility and most of the good people of our town would never stop to think that it might be a rational idea to lock the door when leaving home. Why would you do that? The only consequence of locking the house would be the owners' inconvenience in having to unlock it again upon returning. And on the few occasions I can remember my parents locking our house when we left for a longer trip than just going shopping, the key was invariably left in such an obvious place as to render the locked door irrelevant.

Businesses did lock-up for the night, however. Part of my job during high school at J.C. Penney (a local unit of a national department store chain) was to sweep the store and the front sidewalk before anyone else arrived for the business day. One time I managed to leave the keys inside when I went out past the self-locking front door to tend the sidewalk.

The town's policeman had to be called to break into the store from the back alley so that I could be squeezed through a small (I was teenage skinny then) window to retrieve the keys. I think the town, usually, had only one policeman on duty at a time, although in due course that may have grown to two or three. Of course, there was also the county sheriff with his little jail hidden among our leafy streets, just off the Square (and now a store selling the crafts of local artisans).

I'm not trying to imply that small town Iowans were not security conscious, however. All small Iowa towns exhibited not only tribalism, but a thinly vailed xenophobia as well. Winterset denizens always had a keen nose for 'outsiders,' and the sight of strangers set off inner alarms. Strangers were okay on the town Square where they may have been tourists helping out the local economy. But if they ventured too far, or for too long, into our neighborhoods one's antennae shot up. It seems unlikely that everyone in a town of around 3,500 souls could know everyone else, but anyone in Winterset could tell you instantly if that guy sitting on the park bench *belonged* in town or not. And our keen memories also extended to automobiles. A strange car could set off inner alarm bells, especially if it was parked for too long a time in one spot.

As a young clergyman serving my first parish church in another small Iowa town, in the western part of the state, I vividly recall the dentist's wife, a parishioner, setting me straight on race relations. (I was a hopeless liberal, and one of those rarely encountered, at that time, Democrats.)

She advised me how frightening and unsafe it was for women like her to drive into Omaha (or even into much smaller Sioux City) because when the lady stopped at a gas station, a "Negro" would probably surreptitiously jump into the car trunk, only to jump back out when the lady pulled into her own driveway—and rape her, or worse. (Contrary to her intention, however, the only lesson I took away from her story was that elderly white women might evaluate their remaining sexual attractiveness a tad too highly.)

Whether the women of Winterset were burdened by similar fears of driving into Des Moines I somehow doubt—at least I never heard anyone express a hesitation to drive to our 'big city', which indeed did harbor folks of various ethnic and racial persuasions. But then, Des Moines was only 30 or so miles away, and one could drive there and back home again easily on one tank of gas. So our Winterset women must have cannily figured out that if they set out with a full tank of gas from a local (safe) filling station, at least one urban threat could be totally avoided. And besides, our women

## A Town for All Seasons

were of hearty and brave stock, the daughters of self-reliant farmers give or take a generation. Although they were definitely Iowa Nice, no one would be rash enough to jump into their car trunks in any case.

Municipal services, lavish as they must have been imagined to be by the tax payers, did not include garbage collection. Instead, folks either had to take their garbage out to the town dump themselves, or hire one of the guys who made a little business of collecting trash and taking it to the same dump.

The town dump was an always ablaze and smoking pit which one passed while driving out to the town's man-made lake (water reservoir) and/or the country club.

Young boys (and I guess girls, for that matter, although there were fewer job opportunities for girls) had to wait until age 16 before they could try to land a part-time job. In the meantime, the guys earned their pocket change by pursuing the tasks which were almost full-blown rites-of-passage in small town Iowa: mowing lawns and delivering newspapers. I did both.

My dad may have provided the lawn mowing genes, because he had been a physical worker type guy all his life, first on the farm and then in the machine shops of Greenfield and Winterset.

The newspaper delivery genes probably came from my mother. When her brother was ill for a period, she had taken over his *Omaha World Herald* route in Greenfield, and promptly won a trip to the Chicago World's Fair in a contest to sign up more subscribers.

The lawn mowing device of choice (because early-on there were no options) was a hand-pushed mower. These push-mowers then had a canvas basket attached (at least if one were a 'professional' mower, as were we boys doing it for pay). The basket had to be emptied occasionally, which introduced the problem of where to deposit the freshly cut grass—into a garbage can ideally, but often of necessity under a hedge or some other hidden cover. It would be fun to know now how many miles of walking I did behind a hand mower in my day.

Eventually power lawn mowing machines started appearing and at that point my grandfather rigged up a working motor for me on the carcass of an old push-mower. Suddenly my business was automated, and noisy. I doubt it was any speedier, however. One still had to walk meticulously over every inch of every lawn.

In due course I had a partner (i.e. a friend who shared mowing the lawns with me) whom I annoyed greatly because even when the particular mowing job was not yet finished, I would always insist on going back home to watch the day's episode of 'Captain Video and his Video Rangers' on our fledgling TV set and offered by the soon to be defunct early Dumont television network. Or even before that, to break religiously to hear an episode of one of the radio series about cowboys or Royal Canadian Mounted Police which I seem to have adored. Who could dare accuse me of not having discipline and structure in my life.

Another character trait of the upstanding people of Winterset, was that everyone (almost) was a Republican. As was often the case in my childhood, my Uncle Scotty was the renegade; the only Democrat I knew of or ever heard about in town, although there must have been others, perhaps "under cover" for their own protection. My own later orientation to the Democrats may have begun even earlier than I ever realized, having been born in Adair County as was Henry A. Wallace, the only Iowan ever to hold elective national office as a member of that party.

Now, since the age of Trump has glared down on our national landscape, I feel I must define and defend these Winterset Republicans of yore. They were good, solid, well-intentioned people. They were small-time capitalists and patriots. Although always leery about citizens who lived on "welfare" from the county or state, they would likely give anyone the shirts off their backs without much hesitation. And they were entrepreneurs, as was I with my lawn mowing and snow shoveling businesses. Being a Republican then was a far different matter than could be described of a 21st century Trump party loyalist. A lot has changed between mid-twentieth century America and our nearly mid-twenty-first century country.

Winterset in those days was a real and lively market town, despite being close to Des Moines. Now it seems to be just a bedroom community for Des Moines, almost a suburb. Most residents now seem to work thirty-some miles away in the big town, and seemingly most of the stores on the Square are now filled with cheap antiques or cheap souvenirs rather than the basics of life. But there is still a bakery, I noticed recently, although the clothing stores are now mostly gone. Happily, the little Iowa Theatre still hoists its marquee above John Wayne Drive, still runs current hit movies, and now offers even some live theater.

On one trip home to visit my mother during her nursing home days, I was thrilled to find an actual book store on the town Square. I was so moved I went in to buy several books which I didn't really need nor especially want, at full market rate just to help the cause of the small shop—which, by the way, did not last very much longer despite my effort. Now we're probably back to not even being able to buy a copy of the day's *Des Moines Register* on the Square, a situation which has frustrated me many times over many years. (Copies were usually available in vending machines at the edge of town, but that was too 'suburban' for my taste.)

## A Town for All Seasons

In its day, Winterset stood proudly on its own legs. During the days I worked on the Square as a grocery bagger and carry-out boy, or at J. C. Penny as clerk, window decorator, and stock boy, I can count from memory three grocery supermarkets plus at least five neighborhood grocery stores, two of which were almost candidates for the supermarket league. Plus, an empty store-front building with two display windows perched in a residential neighborhood location and right on the sidewalk rather than set back from it as were all the houses. As a boy I always dreamed of renting it and opening a store, selling heaven-knows-what.

On the courthouse Square we had a bakery, a candy maker, two and sometimes more cafes, a fully functioning movie theatre (as I keep noting, probably because it seemed such a luxury), two drugstores, a couple of women's clothing and a couple of men's clothing stores, plus at least one general clothing store, a couple of five-and-dime variety stores, an auto supply store, some appliance stores, etc. Off-square you could find two or three auto dealers nearby. The local weekly newspaper was actually printed just off the square (I say "actually" because for years now it's been printed in another county, and only written in Winterset by a tiny staff).

As a child going through my first newspaper phase I stopped into *The Madisonian* once to ask for a printing block, and was given a block featuring a tin of Folger's Coffee, and then (contrary to the prevailing generosity and toleration of little kids asking for stuff) was told never to come back begging again. What I saw there, however, amazed me: the guy I talked with kept right on typing, copying from another paper while he spoke with me—wow, this was really sophisticated stuff, and happening right here in Winterset!

While I never figured out how to write stories for my own little newspaper which were centered on a tin of Folger's Coffee for illustration, the little wooden block with a thin metal strip nailed to the top became a valued possession for a newspaper-loving school boy. Actually I could not have used it to illustrate my paper anyway, because my press consisted only of what was then called a hectograph: a flat pan of gelatinous stuff which, when set, could absorb and then release again purple images made on it from a special pencil.

A master copy was made by writing one's text with this special pencil on a sheet of white paper. Then the master copy would be placed face-down on the jelly. When another sheet of white paper was, in turn, placed on the jelly's surface, it would emerge with a purple image of the original. Production time was a little on the slow side, but since the jelly could deliver only three or four copies before they became so faded as to be unreadable, the process probably did not really require speed. And circulation was miniscule, so a total run of three or four copies did the job nicely.

## PENNEY'S ON THE SQUARE

Saturday evening in Winterset was the big market night, crowded with folks who had come into town to shop for their week's need of food and clothing. Anyone who had a store job (which was most of the in-town working population because the main industry was retail) worked late on Saturday. By the time I was an upper classman in high school, I had a job I liked and which carried real responsibility at (J. C.) 'Penney's. I did almost everything there was to be done at the store except to count the money. Actually, one of my classmates landed the job first, but had to bow out when the management learned he was only fifteen. Being a few months older than my friend, I then had the opportunity to profiteer from his loss, and I was accepted; a gigantic step in the newly pressing matter of growing up.

Way up on the top floor, above the balcony where Mr. Penner, my boss, would sit surveying his domain while doing book work, was a room with very large tables where the national chain's decorating and advertising materials were stored and worked out. I got the job of setting up the prescribed window displays, which no one else wanted and I was deliriously happy to have.

I had to remove my shoes to go into the window space so that nothing got tracked into the display which sometimes involved white paper or cloth on the floor. Somehow this felt almost risqué whenever my current "girlfriend" would come by to watch the process unfolding from outside the window, with me in my stocking feet.

But on Saturday evenings all hands were needed on the sales floor. One such evening a customer (clearly a farmer on shopping duty) came in wearing overalls (hopefully you need no explanation even if you're not from Iowa) and needing another pair. We carried such things in spades, of course. Ours were proudly "Sanforized," which was a trade name for a process which protected the cloth from much shrinking. As I was helping the farmer with his overalls purchase, he turned to me and asked, "Now, you're sure they're pasteurized, right?"

Another big evening in Winterset during the summer was when the high school band gave concerts on the town Square. We would set up on one of the four big porches of the cruciform shaped court house (always the west porch; see below) and offer a program of accessible, not-at-all-challenging fare.

## A Town for All Seasons

There were always a few audience people scattered around the lawn, mostly on the several benches afforded there. But the biggest part of the audience, in true Winterset custom, sat inside their autos parked around the Square—their true level of musical connoisseurship demonstrated by their lack of concern for the diminished acoustical circumstances thereby self-imposed.

The cute Winterset thing about it, though, was that this audience applauded by honking their car horns—many times after each piece on the program, probably making more noise for their compatriot car dwellers than had been heard from the band by any of them in the first place.

One of my favorite stories about the Square came courtesy of a classmate. He got his public spotlight moment because we high schoolers were all just in the process of learning how to control an automobile.

There were two five-and-dime stores in town: Ben Franklin's where I worked many a summer vacation from college, and Harrison's, which was owned by this friend's father. They were located on the same side of the Square, probably only about three or four doors from each other.

One fine day Larry, our classmate, was trying to park in one of the angled head-in spaces allowed on the street; most likely he was on his way to Harrison's. The parking space he found open was directly in front of Ben Franklin's. Parking around the Square was controlled by parking meters set on top of poles in front of each parking space and into which one put nickels or dimes to buy time.

The meters may not have been as carefully attached to their support poles as would have been desirable. In some kind of novice error, Larry must have stepped on the gas rather than the brake—wham!—he hit the pole, and its meter flew into a plate glass display window—belonging to, you guessed it, Ben Franklin's. I'm happy to report that no one was injured, but the window had certainly seen better days.

The Ben Franklin store was owned and operated by friends of my parents, with whom they had grown up in Greenfield in the next county. Before buying a big house in the west end of town, they lived in one of the apartments over their store, which was true of many store owners on the Square in their young adult days.

*South side of the Winterset Square showing the Ben Franklin store and next to it the former J.C. Penney store, two of the three stores on the Square where the author worked as a teenager (photo: Teddi Yaeger)*

It was in this upstairs apartment that I, as a very young child, probably humiliated my parents without having the faintest clue I might be doing so. Their friends' relatives were visiting from Greenfield, where the relatives also ran a Ben Franklin store. My brother and I were playing on the floor while the grown-ups talked. Out of the blue, to my memory at least, the grandmother figure in the room asked us what we were hoping Santa would bring us; it must have been near Christmas. Without hesitation, and certainly without any forethought, I joyously replied that I wanted a doll for Christmas.

The doll arrived as promised. I was still innocent of any reason I should feel guilty about wanting and having a doll, although there was a very faint whisper in the back of my mind somewhere which suggested that this might not be a typical boy thing to want.

Anyway, I named her Marianne despite her having a penis. I don't think she was intended to have that particular anatomical feature because she lacked the double attachment that normally comes along with having a penis. Probably the penis was the result of a coating which ran a bit before setting during the doll's manufacture. It was my Uncle Scotty who first spotted the doll's anomaly and constantly expounded loudly on the subject whenever I played with Marianne in his presence.

I once held a birthday party for Marianne when I was sick at home and not able to attend school—during first grade probably. I laid out various treats for this party, including a chocolate bar broken up into its pre-marked little squares. The preacher showed up unannounced to visit my mother, and I asked from my sickbed that he be invited to Marianne's birthday party. He declined. My mother explained after he left that he probably just did not want to be exposed to my illness.

*Sure.* That *had* to be the reason. Clergymen otherwise just love to attend doll parties thrown by little boys who should instead be pushing little toy trucks around on the floor and articulating motor noises. But Marianne eventually died (I guess, she disappeared anyway) and I was indeed reduced finally to pushing toy trucks around on the floor like any other boys my age—one of them, a plastic pick-up truck model, so realistic and cherished that it lives on still in an old man's memory.

## WEST, TOWARD DENVER

West was Winterset's orientation of choice; Denver was its direction of yearning—perhaps some affection, or at least curiosity, was left-over for brawny Chicago, but who needed effete New York and the East (except me, and maybe any other boy or girl of similar constitution if they were hiding anywhere in town unbeknownst to me)? No, it was westward-ho, and once you retired you didn't stop until you got to California (populated with at least one city I'd heard of which was made up almost entirely of retired and transplanted Iowans).

We were compatriots of Josiah B. Grinnell, the recipient of the famous advice to "Go west, young man, go west." Grinnell followed the advice but made it only as far as central Iowa. His fellow Iowans looked and yearned further west.

This western orientation was a built-in part of Iowa's natural identity. The Iowa Territory before statehood had been a vast area covering several of today's western states. From our Mississippi River eastern boundary we always looked west. At one point the catholic bishop of Dubuque had a diocese which stretched all the way to California's eastern border, I'm told, but in any case it covered a big portion of our continental footprint. The first U.S. president born west of the Mississippi was a native Iowan. The Mormon wagon trains on their way to Utah had crossed our territory, pulling our attention westward again. We were simply westerners, and many of us dressed the part stereotypically with 'cowboy' hats and boots.

## Winterset In Time

West was the direction of aspiration in Winterset, as it was also in most of the Midwestern towns and cities, of that era. The most prosperous merchants lived in the 'West End' in big (for Winterset) houses with large (for Winterset) lawns. These folks belonged to the country club.

The eastern (or at least, non-western) half of town always could have used a new coat of paint, and its denizens usually did not belong to the country club.

Both of the houses in which I grew up were located just on the railroad tracks, so it was somewhat difficult to know if we were on the right or wrong side of the tracks. But we were face-savingly on the side closest to the Square, and therefore to the desirable West End.

My newspaper delivery days for the *Des Moines Tribune* (an afternoon paper, now deceased), however, involved a route decidedly on the wrong side of the tracks—peeling houses, angry dogs, mobile homes no longer mobile, dead cars left on the front yard, scads of usually barefoot and often dirty children playing on front porches. And folks who thought reading a newspaper was a more intellectual pursuit than they were cut out for. Plus a smaller group who were happy to subscribe to the newspaper but who were often surprised when collection day came around and sometimes in need of asking for an extension until the following week.

I'd have to observe, however, that the 'non-west end' of town has improved greatly since my newspaper delivery days. Also, my brother built his house there and raised my niece and nephew there, and his house became my non-official headquarters in Winterset as adulthood rooted me in other places, always east coast places. I understood the western pull but it was never sufficient to make me face west—some would feel that I was oriented to the past by wanting to be an easterner, while the rest of Iowa was oriented to the future by yearning for the glorious west.

Winterset is the sort of place one never really leaves. The periods between visits home may become longer and longer, but one is always there somehow in one's heart. And one is never without Winterset's formational influence even if one has taken up residence in the wicked East, or if Fifth Avenue is now one's Main Street.

In my own big city life in the eastern (I'm sorry, Winterset, not in the western) part of the country, I've run across many people who are ready at the drop of a hat to besmirch their home towns or states of origin in derisive discussion. They'd grown too big for their britches, as we Iowans would probably say, and ashamed of their less sophisticated, less urban, beginnings.

But I've never met people from Iowa who would dream of doing that. I've met plenty of people in the east who were originally from Iowa, but they retain an almost religious loyalty to "home." We may live in New York (or Philadelphia, or wherever) now, but we're still Iowans. I can travel nowhere wearing my University of Iowa "I" cap without someone asking about home—in the Paris metro; wherever.

So great big grown-up me, educated and (hopefully) sophisticated, and comfortable with the ways of the world—I'm still from Winterset, I'm still an Iowan, and I'm still proud of it. ⌘

## ABOUT THE DEDICATEE

All of this Iowa niceness we've considered—did much of it rub off on me, you may rightly ask? I'd have to admit that I'm not the nicest person in my family. That distinction without any equivocation belongs to my husband, John. But at least my training in Iowa niceness helped me greatly in knowing what to look for in a life partner.

Then the question becomes, why is John so nice? I think the answer is obvious. He may have been born in Georgia, but part of his childhood was spent in Illinois.

Now, look at a map. Illinois is snuggling up to Iowa with only a ribbon of blue separating them. If you are in Illinois a mere river separates you from the epicenter of niceness: Iowa. So John had no choice really. Living, if only for a few years, so close to Iowa was enough to implant niceness in him permanently.

And another clue. John loves Iowa and is always ready to travel there, even sometimes when I'm not sure if I'm up for the trip myself. Football in Iowa City? Count him in. State Fair? Yeah, let's go again this year. Winterset? Every street has already been memorized, but that's no reason to forego the pleasure yet again. Maybe it's actually John who is the real Iowan in our family. At any rate, he's the nicest person in our family, and that's already meeting the primary qualification for being a true Iowan. ⌘

# Postscript 1:
# Acquiring an Adjective in a Place Like Winterset

I really hated adding the tag line to the title of this book. Or at least needing to include one little three letter word in it.

I'd hoped to write just about growing up in Winterset. The town itself should have been the star of the story. Yet I could not extract myself from the story either, and my story was a little different from that of most, or maybe even all, of my childhood friends.

Had I been of the same sexuality as most other people in town at the time, it probably would not even have occurred to me that a growing fondness for girls was anything but a happy and natural chapter everyone would want to read about, and expect to read about.

But my story, unfortunately, lacked a growing fondness for girls. And in our world, at least as it was constituted back then, that automatically became a big part of the story on its own.

The problem comes in being part of a minority.

If one is part of the majority, one's sexuality does not define one. It might even just blend into the background. It's just a given. A given which everyone assumes, which one does not even have to state or point out, and which no one feels contains anything in need of forgiveness or toleration or even further explanation. About the only adjectives a white heterosexual man may encounter along the way is a joyous "young" man early on, gradually yielding to a somewhat less welcome "old" man in due course.

But if one is part of a minority, one is suddenly not *merely* a man. One acquires an adjective.

One is a *Black* man, for example, or a *handicapped* man. Or, a *gay* man. An adjective is now attached to one's core being. Being part of a minority elevates the contrast with the majority into a defining mark. A Scarlet Letter, as it were. So my adjective forced itself into the story and gave the story its unique color. I can't see any honest way to have avoided that without turning my story into fiction.

No one volunteers to be part of a racial or sexual minority. Nature decides, and then sits back to watch the individual cope. Ironically I did not really know I was in the minority (despite quite a few hints) until long after I had left Winterset; I just had something unsettled in the back of my head which kept suggesting that something significantly important was off kilter.

But at the moment of unavoidable recognition, not only the future changes, but the past also.

One can no longer pretend that the signs were not there all along. One can no longer read one's past as a litany of purely innocent ignorance. Explanations pop into place. A pattern emerges; a pattern which cannot be divorced from one's life either past, present, or future. So telling one's story honestly takes on a new burden. Even a retroactive burden.

A straight guy writing about his childhood probably would not even pause to realize that he was also writing about his sexuality. Sexuality is just part of life. He would not be defined as a *heterosexual* boy, just as a *boy* growing up. No adjectives needed.

When the boy is not heterosexual, however, the story changes because all the assumptions change.

The choice becomes whether to tell an honest story, or to fabricate a hollow story. In this attempt to tell my Winterset story I came to realize the time expended was not worth the effort if it were not honest. And if it were not honest, there would be costs attached—just one small example: I'd sacrifice the possibility of being helpful to some anonymous gay kid struggling to grow up in an American small town who might stumble upon this book. That alone was too big a price to pay.

Sexuality or sexual orientation is not anyone's whole story. Each of us is much bigger than that. Yet sexuality is part of each of our stories. There is no way to escape that.

To tell one's story requires that one does not attempt to pretend to be anything beyond what one actually is. At least if one hopes to remain just this side of fiction.

So I gradually came to accept that I could not write simply about a boy growing up in Winterset; my only option was to write about a gay boy growing up in Winterset. I leave writing the other story to the straight boys who grew up beside me there. I hope there are some who take up the challenge, and I hope I don't miss out on reading their contributions. I'd really like to have a clue about what my story would have felt like had I been one of my straight friends.

Every gay boy—at least back in the less worldly-wise middle of the 20th century—was condemned to go through the terror of a period of torture. He was afraid he could be the only human who was failing to live up to the dictates of the Creator, and destined to crush the hopes of his parents on top of that. Down the road there was some relief waiting when he discovered he was part of a large fraternity—by no means the only one in the world, although perhaps still at risk of defying Divine Providence and

# Postscript 1

causing suffering to those who loved him. It got better, but the torture did not vanish like magic.

They say things are getting better for gay kids these days, and it seems like that's mostly true. But no one escapes related growing pains. Being 'different,' being part of a minority, simply does not fit into the way we want to relate to each other.

And it's always painful even if we try hard to bury the pain and keep it at arm's length. Humans are social creatures, and anything which enforces artificial separation causes pain of some kind. This postscript may seem a bit clunky and maybe even out of place, but I add it for the sake of any young gay readers who may happen upon this book. I add it so that my peers from back then can have a better understanding of some of their friends who didn't seem to quite fit in. And I add it because my generation has its own legitimate perspective to express, just like those before and those which will follow.

Looking back on my school days from the perspective of an adult, I must have daydreamed thousands of times about my peers back then and, again, wondered if I was "the only one."

If you, like me, grew up in a small Midwestern town in those days, you will appreciate that topics such as this were simply off the table, at least until after high school for most of us. So those of us who went on to a wider world quickly after high school, leaving our home town at the first viable opportunity, are probably doomed to do nothing more than continue to speculate. Statistically there could have been a handful of gay guys in my high school graduating class, but if so none of us were really sure just what was happening to us at that point. And we were certainly not going to risk talking to anyone about it. That's just not how Winterset operated back then.

To the extent I have learned about the adult lives of my most remembered friends from high school, they all seem to have married and most of them became parents. That is as much of a clue as I have, although by now we also understand that such clues do not necessarily accurately portray the realities of life in all cases. So I remain curious. Curious, and secretly hopeful that one of my classmates may come across this book and find a way to contact me with the news that I was, in fact, not the only one.

I do know now, however, that one of the closest companions from my childhood was cut of the same material as was I. My brother and I had only two first cousins, and I really knew only the eldest because his brother was so much younger than were we. But cousin Jimmy was a fixture of my childhood. He visited Iowa every summer to spend a few weeks in

Greenfield with our grandparents, and sometimes would even be driven the 20 or so miles over to Winterset to stay with us for a week.

Mostly I remember playing with him for hours on the big swing hanging in our grandparents' shady front porch, and most vividly working endlessly on the jig-saw puzzle wherein we had to place all 48 lower states in the proper proximity to each other. It was luxuriating in the complete innocence of childhood. Any birds and bees stayed in the garden where they belonged.

Jimmy was a couple years younger than me, but he was an urban kid so perhaps it is no surprise that he figured out the birds and the bees before I did—or at least that our particular birds and bees were of a somewhat different stripe than those of our brothers. Perhaps unfortunately, this revelation had to wait for the cusp of adulthood so we were not able to lend support to each other during the more vulnerable growing up years.

Then as an adult he surprised me again, living out the social equality I was preaching about from the Lutheran pulpit of another small Iowa town. He acquired his life's companion in New York City, a Black man he later described to me as "the kindest, most gentle human I have ever met."

I think they were a solid couple who would have eventually married had Jimmy lived long enough. When Jimmy's parents prevailed on him to return home to Buffalo because of some help they thought he could render in getting his younger brother through some difficulty, Jimmy's partner made the sacrifice of leaving New York and moving with Jimmy.

Then he was left alone in a city not yet even familiar to him. Jimmy was killed while riding in a car driven by his brother. The car skidded into a bridge abutment on unseen ice. His brother escaped and his wife and infant child were thrown out to safety, but Jimmy was knocked unconscious and perished in flames. I met his partner only at his funeral.

To place a purely selfish spin on what was really a very painful loss, I was now the official black-sheep of our family—the only gay man left standing. There was no longer anyone to share the minority position with. No one left I could be really sure understood me, or even really accepted me.

I had hoped that in retirement, after the hustle and hassle of our working years, we would all be close. I hoped that about my brother too. I imagined the golden years where we would learn to be as close again as we were when children, untroubled by such ultimately unimportant stuff as whether it was a male or a female we were destined by nature to love most dearly. Destiny had other plans though. Both Jimmy and my brother were taken before these retirement years. So too was my gay brother-in-law.

# Postscript 1

So I now have a family of my own, but still wonder about the friends and peers I left in high school. They don't stop mattering just because the years of separation grow more numerous; actually they almost begin to matter more. In a sense I worry about them—were they happy in life? Did they enjoy their time on this orb? Much to my joy I've reconnected with a few. Oddly, maybe, they are some of the girls. Is that a strange symptom of being gay? Do I value the girls more now than I did then? Did I have more in common with the girls even then without recognizing it? Maybe I just couldn't figure out how to be closer to the girls back then.

Living is a mysterious business. I hope I can live long enough to figure it all out, but I'm not betting on that. Few of us do.

Maybe the bottom line is that we're all in the same boat.

If one looks just at the surface of things it may not seem that way. But in the long run does it really matter that some of us were heterosexual and some were not? Yes, in the sense that we as a species need to procreate. No, in the sense that it certainly does not take all of us to accomplish that imperative. And no, too, in that society is beginning to let gay guys and lesbians be parents notwithstanding their handicap of limited sexual adventurousness. In the meantime we're all humans with individual stories and a common fate. I think, ultimately, what mattered is that each of us did find a mate to help us through the pitfalls of life and to celebrate together life's little triumphs along the way. What adjectives may have been attached to that mate were ultimately of minor consequence.

Nevertheless, I'd really enjoy being back in high school having finished the chapter on the birds and the bees—at least I *think* I would. Back in the middle of the 20th century and in small town Iowa, that could also have been absolute hell. Even in a town as overall nice as Winterset. Being "in the closet" was probably ultimately my salvation, even though I may not yet even have understood that was where I was.

So it was that Winterset—any "Winterset"—was both a protective mother to the gay schoolkids growing up under her wings, and a force which blocked reality and delayed self-recognition until the safer shores of near adulthood.

I continue to be grateful to Winterset for a basically untroubled childhood. That foundation served me well when the closet walls collapsed around me and I could no longer hide. It also kept reminding me that things could still get better no matter what trial of life presented itself.

Winterset was not just home, it was a state of mind.

Inside that state of mind things were never completely hopeless, challenging as they may have become. There was always another bright sunny day ahead somewhere which would wipe away any tears of the moment.

Sometimes I daydream a bit about kids living in Winterset right now. Some of them are gay. I've never met any of them but I know they know about themselves. And even if they're still hoping 'it's just a phase,' most of their friends already know anyway.

This is not the 1940s or 1950s anymore.

Is that a blessing for schoolboys who can't work up a passion for their female classmates, try as they might? Maybe.

But they will not be able to look back at the Winterset of their past and feel only its charm and acceptance. They will feel also the sting of rejection, at least to a degree my generation escaped. My grandniece tells me that there was bullying and harassment in evidence for the gay kids she knew before graduating from Winterset High School recently. So Winterset is trying to grow with the times, but may be having a more difficult time doing so than her past tranquility would suggest.

I dedicated this book to my partner/husband of over half a century, not only because he is the light of my life, but because he is the one who suggested I try writing in retirement. Actually, it was more of an order. As I relate in the forward to my first published book, we were in Venice for an extended stay and I, implausibly, was getting bored. And it was specifically this book he wanted me to write, even though I wrote some others first. So there is no question that this book is for John.

If it had not belonged to John in so specific a way, I might have considered dedicating it to the gay Winterset kids of today.

They are anonymous to me, but I know they are there. And as we head toward the middle of the 21$^{st}$ century, they can't escape knowing they're there as well. The vague hazy cover that cloaked such topics in my Winterset days has been ripped away by time and modern communications. So these kids I don't know tug at my heart nonetheless because they have been robbed of the chance to grow up slowly, and in an almost universally accepting context. I also lament that they may look back at their hometown in years to come and remember a place less joyous and less protecting than I've had the gift to remember. ⌘

# Postscript 2:
# On Losing My Brother, a Winterset Fixture

Probably my main claim to fame in Winterset as an adult was that I was the brother of my younger brother. His loss fell outside the chronological scope of my main story here, but I can hardly write about Winterset and omit one of her favorite sons.

He was widely known and widely loved in town as an adult, and he was a native who never left home. He was gregarious and a man of many friends. I, on the other hand, had spent all of my adult life away from Winterset. I was instinctively shy and something of an introvert.

To illustrate my un-Winterset credentials I report that, to my confusion and chagrin, and yet a touch of perverse pride at the same time, I had been turned down for a job at a major New York department store once because I was judged to be "an intellectual." Yes, if you wanted to know one of us, Richard was certainly the right choice for Winterset folks. He was always 'down to earth,' whereas my own feet may have floated a bit from time to time. He was happy to remain tethered to his home town; I'm not even sure one could have blasted him out of it. Whereas I, in a display of apparent uppityness, had put down new roots in large cities on the East Coast.

He studied to become a welder during a brief period at a technical school in Minneapolis, then came home to assist our father in his machine shop business, located about a block off the Winterset square; a business Richard then ran by himself for some additional years after Dad was forced to retire because of Parkinson's Disease.

One of my dad's moments of quiet civic contribution, as I mentioned earlier, was being asked by the Secret Service to construct a metal core for bullet-protection inside a podium to be used when President Ronald Reagan once spoke in Winterset on the courthouse Square.

One of my brother's unsung civic contributions was designing and constructing a propane-fueled device to thaw and open grave sites during Winterset's frequently severe winters. I can't help wondering if his invention was used to open his own grave during that terrible February when one of the local morticians administered his professional services to the fire chief, his long-time buddy.

It was Richard's love of being a volunteer fireman that gave him his place in the heart of, and the hearts of, Winterset. He was the town's fire chief for a total of nineteen years divided into two periods, and a member of the department for much longer than that. And it was this position which afforded him the opportunity to indulge his generous but distinctive personality.

Being a fireman, it seemed to me at a distance, was really what my brother's life was all about. And it was so on a daily basis.

Volunteer firemen in Winterset can still be summoned at any moment, from any activity, or any circumstance, by the wail of the big siren above the fire station and the beeps of the alerting devices they carry around all day.

This was so much the case that Richard disappeared suddenly from the family scene many times during visits I made back to Winterset. I started to wonder if I was the problem somehow; was he glad to have an excuse to leave the scene whenever I was back in town? A least my visits home seemed to be an omen for lots of fires in the area.

And it seemed obvious enough that Richard was obsessed with all this fire-fighting business. A fellow volunteer fireman recalled at Richard's wake that when he (the colleague) became the parent of a little boy, Richard casually mentioned that maybe it was a good thing it wasn't a girl because in that case the guy would have needed to name her "Alexus" (I think that was the word). I gather this was the name, or involved the name, of a line of fire engine trucks, and obviously, any self-respecting fireman of the town and time would instinctively gravitate in that direction to come up with a female sounding name.

One of my favorite scenes in his life, although I was not present to witness it, came about because the filming of the Hollywood version of "The Bridges of Madison County" took place in Winterset and the production needed to enlist Richard's fire department for help. The script called for rain, so the fire trucks sprayed the set and the actors while the cameras rolled, as I've also mentioned earlier.

As a result of the film, Winterset enjoyed a period of being something of a tourist attraction, with lots of visitors both domestic and foreign. Richard, as a genuine local, hung out with his buddies at the North Side Café, then about the only place to eat in town. Tourists likewise flocked to the North Side Café because of the role it played in the movie.

Richard said he was frequently asked by a stranger, "Which stool at the counter did Clint Eastwood sit at?" Then, while having not the faintest clue himself, he would point confidently at one, and say "Why it was that one, right there."

This was pure Richard—the stranger took a photo of the stool and went away happy, and Richard had yet another story in his well-supplied arsenal.

## Postscript 2

Were we close as brothers? Everyone (at least my aunt) said we were as different as night and day, but there were certainly moments of closeness, or at least intense involvement. There was the time, for instance, when during one of our favorite pass times (throwing a ball back and forth over the neighbor's garage through which we could not see each other) he substituted a rock for the ball and nailed me point-blank in the head. Was he laughing over on his hidden side of the garage? All I can remember is running into the house crying and fearing I'd spend the rest of my life as some kind of brain-smushed idiot.

I went to the airport to see him off when he left for military service, as a good brother should have done. And later when I wrote to him out of panic from my first parish assignment he came as soon as he could to visit, as a good brother should have done. (I was suffering greatly from the gay thing and trying to fit it into my new position as a clergyman who could preach only the church's official take on everything, and I was desperate to unburden myself to someone.)

I remember writing to him something like "Mom and Dad raised me differently than they raised you." The currently popular theory was that homosexuality was caused by nurture rather than nature, and the theory was full of stuff like emotionally distant fathers and over-protective mothers—factors which almost any gay guys could discern in their backgrounds if they looked hard enough, whether warranted or not.

So Richard came as beckoned—but I chickened out of telling him anything of which I'd hoped to unburden myself. Soon enough he had it all figured out anyway.

When Richard married I was there again, as a good brother should have been. He didn't need me as a best man or any of the usual brother roles because he was rich with close friends from school days. I was a relatively freshly minted clergyman, so I shared presiding duties with the Methodist minister in Winterset, leaving my mark on the day and the lives of the bride and groom by signing the marriage certificate as a sanctioned representative of the state of Iowa. And in turn I was rewarded by not having to come up with a clever speech to deliver at the reception.

Then they, Richard and Diane, were off to Louisiana to complete his military service and to start the process of giving me a niece, while I was off to New York where I'd just been named pastor of a church in the most unflatteringly storied reaches of the South Bronx.

Should I admit that I found one of the groomsmen fairly attractive and spent as much time as I could talking with him at the rehearsal dinner and reception? Should I admit that after the wedding and before moving to New York I drove back to Omaha to keep an overnight date with a young guy I met in my last few days stationed at my first parish assignment? It was clear my life and my brother's were heading off in greatly different directions.

The New York years saw my brother and I gradually drift apart. He and Diane never visited me there. They visited only once, later, in New Jersey, along with our parents, but not during my many years in Connecticut later still. Of course, they were raising a family now, and both time and money were needed for more immediate purposes than travel to the East Coast (although I'm sorry they never capitalized on having a free bed and a free travel guide in the East back then).

I tried to get to Winterset as often as I could while my parents were still alive, and of course that meant some family time with my brother and his crew on each trip. Later, when these trips were necessitated by what seemed to be funeral after funeral, I was almost always a dinner guest of Richard and Diane at their Winterset house. Still there was an underlying tension which never eased and probably was getting worse.

Maybe Richard thought I felt I was too good for him now. I'd gone to university, the first to do so in our family, although Richard could have also if he'd wanted. I now lived in one big Eastern city or another. I was a "professional" white collar type even after I was a Roman collar type. I probably let slip hints of a love for music or art; trips to the opera or other activities which went underappreciated by most Winterset standards. I travelled in Europe frequently. I could not effectively hide being gay, although we never talked about it in direct terms. In short, maybe I was not Winterset enough anymore. Maybe, as a good Iowan would say, I'd grown 'too big for my britches'.

And worst of all, I couldn't avoid leaving continuing hints that I was gay, try as I might to neutralize that side of things. I was not living with a woman; I was living with a man. How does one cover that over without giving up all honesty? And brothers were not meant to be that dishonest with each other—besides our parents had figured things out, largely because they did visit John and me several times during that period. Anyway I could feel the chill creeping into my relationship with Richard and as much as I hated that, I had no idea what to do about it.

When Richard was near death with pancreatic cancer and we'd at least resumed frequent telephone conversations because of his illness, I asked my sister-in-law if I should come back to Winterset to see him. She said, "Yes, I think you'd better come back." I knew what she meant—Richard did not have much time left.

But she never knew what I was *really* asking—would my presence upset him at this time when he needed peace? Would the insertion of a distant,

## Postscript 2

and gay, brother into those fraught days be at all welcome? I didn't want to visit him at his deathbed and go away feeling guilty that I'd ruined some of his precious last hours. I pictured myself by then as mostly a thorn in his side; a figure to be tolerated only because of blood.

I visited him in his Des Moines hospital room during his last treatment days—he was terminal, as the code on his door hammered into me at every entrance. We had better conversations than might have been expected in those circumstances. I soldiered through visits by his brother Winterset firemen, long talks with Diane about their family life while Richard napped, and the smothering agony of it all.

But Richard at that point was living solely in anticipation of going home to Winterset one last time. "I may not last long after I get there," he told his firefighting buddies, "but I'm going home." He did go home, and he didn't last long there as he predicted; just one overnight.

When his doctors finally okayed the transfer, they scheduled an ambulance to carry him to Winterset hospital. "No," said the Winterset firemen, "he's ours". They dispatched their own ambulance, with its own crew of Richard's friends, to drive to Des Moines to pick him up for that final trip home. Along the way, they stopped at a store somewhere to buy Richard's favorite flavor of pop.

In the Winterset hospital parking lot waiting for this ambulance and observing the gathering fire equipment there to greet Richard upon his return home, the display of love by his peers brought surprising and chocking sobs, and my eyes teared for the first time in years. I was overwhelmed that Winterset loved him so deeply, and I was feeling so many layers of my own loss. I called my husband-to-be and sobbed into the phone; "I'm crying, too" he whispered back to me.

Richard and his wife were sure to visit us at least when retirement rolled around (his wife did visit us in Florida for a lovely week a year after his death). If they visited us in Hartford, we would drive them to the fire fighters' museum not far away in New York's antiques town Hudson. We would sit around over beers (for him) and wine (for the rest of us) and learn to know each other again—and the friction would disappear and he and Diane and John and I would be great friends. Maybe we'd even vacation together as travelers.

That lovely period of reconciliation never arrived, however. He died out of sequence before he could retire, and I was robbed. I was not the only one robbed, of course; he had a wife, two children, and four grandchildren. But I was robbed twice—he was my brother, and he was my brother who needed to accept his brother completely again whether gay or not. My grand reconciliation flew away into the night, leaving yet another cause for tears.

The morning after Richard returned to Winterset I asked the medical people at the hospice desk in the hospital how they assessed the situation. I was not yet retired, and I was much in need of the comfort of the people I loved back in Hartford. The hospice desk estimated that he would linger for a few days—maybe even a couple of weeks.

I couldn't stay indefinitely in Winterset, especially not knowing how long would be necessary. Better to go home and then return when it was time, even if that would be soon. Driving on the way to Des Moines airport, my cell phone rang. It was my niece. I asked her to give me time to pull off the highway before giving me the news that I knew she now must deliver.

Still, I was the last family member to speak with my brother on his death bed; everyone had scattered for their work week duties except my niece, whom I asked to give me and Richard a private moment by waiting in a near-by lounge.

The right words are never obvious in that situation, so I took my cue from my wise husband's attempt to comfort his own younger brother at another death bed. I simply held his hand and said "Take your rest." Something passed between us. There were no more words but somehow I think it may have been the reconciliation which I'd scheduled for later over leisurely drinks and under much happier skies.

But maybe, and blessedly, it was only the last part of the reconciliation process I'd hoped for. My sister-in-law later told me that she had only seen Richard cry twice during their marriage—once when our father died, and once after Richard and I finished our last telephone conversation. "We should have visited Phil," he told her. Maybe we were already reconciled when I touched his hand for the last time.

In that telephone conversation I had been telling him about the Orange Bowl game just past where John and I had gone to watch Iowa defeat Georgia Tech. It came during one of those cold snaps which can surprise everyone in South Florida, and this one was a real doozy. Only the visiting Iowans could cope with it easily; they, after all, were veterans of such temperatures at that time of year.

It was so damn cold that John and I left during half-time to drive back to our Florida home and watch the second half on TV. "We swore to keep that secret," I told my brother, "but I suppose I can tell you." Perhaps Richard caught a vision of me as an actual real-life human being which he had not seen for many years; a fairly ordinary American man eagerly going to a football game but humanly vulnerable just like other folks. Perhaps he

## Postscript 2

regretted, as he seemed to tell Diane, that we had grown apart. Perhaps he suddenly saw me as not being all that far from a regular guy after all.

I do know he was touched during our phone calls by one of the most simple things I mentioned. Evidently I made some kind of reference to the Iowa Firefighters' Convention he had organized and hosted years earlier and I mentioned the two souvenir commemorative coffee mugs from the event he had mailed to me then. Richard expressed great surprise that we still had them, and I said yes, we use them daily. His surprise, pride, and flash of affection was apparent even over phone wires. I use and treasure these mugs still.

My gay cousin Jimmy died out of sequence too, as I've mentioned to you, and I miss him; he was supposed to be my single gay family compatriot in older age. I'm very lucky to have a loving husband and several top-notch friends, including a younger housemate who looks after me as if he were my son. But at least three key players—my brother, my brother-in-law, and my cousin Jimmy—are missing and that hurt never entirely goes away. The play now has to go on with a rewritten third act and a smaller cast.

Yes, Richard was supposed to be part of my life in retirement—one is always robbed of part of one's own future when someone close dies out of sequence.

Groups of Richard's family and friends crowded into the hospice room at Winterset hospital. The firemen regaled themselves and us with oh-so-many stories of the Fire Chief in action. No one mentioned aloud the great tragedy of Richard's reign, when a young recruit had been killed in an explosion while they were fighting a town fire. This was the time for a lighter touch they seemed to feel, as they told of exploits like the time coming back from a rural fire that the whole hundreds of feet of hose flew off the back of a fire engine because a newbie had folded it incorrectly.

They told of Richard's giving the finger to a passenger car which was blocking his trucks from making needed time to a fire. They said he had shouted "This is my road, get out of the way!" (the real words actually may have been a tad spicier than that) as the offending car was finally passed. Richard said from his bed, "I could tell that story the right way, but I'm a little tired now." It was the last time he'd speak of fires in Winterset. Maybe it was even the last time he spoke at all.

Richard's funeral was a dramatic telling of the love his town held for its fire chief. And I somehow had managed to attempt to add my bit of love and tribute then as well.

My Niece had become the family's eulogy presenter after giving stirring remembrances for my mother and for my Aunt Ina. But this time, for her dad, she must have felt she could not pull it off. As we sat in the Lutheran church planning the funeral, no one volunteered to speak in public. I felt it was only right and proper that there should be something said about Richard by a family member, so I somewhat hesitatingly volunteered out of a sense of duty, and out of a sense of loyalty to a man I loved but hardly knew any more.

Longtime Winterset Fire Chief Richard Truckenbrod embraced by his wife Diane at the Fire House circa 2010 (Photo: LeAnn Tucker)

I had enough time to compose a relatively contained tribute which I kept honing and memorizing. When the sad time came, I was able to deliver it from memory and felt that it probably came across to the mourners decently. Later, at the grave site, in front of the wreath of roses I had contributed with its diagonal red ribbon proclaiming "Brother," one of Diane's brothers came over to speak with me. "Richard was really lucky to have a brother like you," he said with obvious sincerity. I was shocked, thinking of the years I was sure Richard was so disappointed in me. But at least it gave me hope that I had, indeed, given him the worthy family tribute he deserved.

The funeral was sprinkled with firing squad salutes from veterans' groups, the bell ringing codes from the early New York City fire communications system that indicated a man had been lost, and lots of tales from Winterset firemen told with jocular stiff upper lips. The fire department guys showed us the 'trophies' Richard made in his basement workshop and delivered to 'winners' at the annual firefighters' banquets— trophies like the one designated for the "dumbest-ass miscue of the year" by a local fireman.

Then we followed Richard on his last ride. It was fast tradition at a fireman's funeral for the coffin to be hoisted to the back of a fire engine for the trip to the cemetery, with an honor guard of the man's colleagues standing on the truck's back bumper and in uniform. Winterset had only one actual formal fire uniform, but it was worn with dignity and affection as Richard was escorted through the town's streets.

## Postscript 2

Richard's stories and practical jokes were now finished—except for one my niece's husband told again *en route* to the cemetery. Richard had proposed that he record the message, "Hey, be careful. Don't drop me," and that the recording device be geared to sound when tilted and then finally placed by some conspirator inside his casket, awaiting the moment when the firemen would hoist his casket onto the back of the engine for the ride to the cemetery. It was just as well that this plot never left the planning stages, although again—it would have been pure Richard.

*The chief and his wife on his last Christmas with daughter Lori's family on the right and son Jason's family on the left (Photo: LeAnn Tucker)*

We passed under a gigantic American flag hung from the extended ladders of a fire engine on each side of the street at the Square, in front of Ben Franklin's. Winterset was saying good-bye to a local hero.

I was exhausted after the burial. I'd honored my brother in whatever little way I could. It was now time to reassemble at the fire hall for a lunch given by the firemen's wives. It was time for less somber talk. For yet more tales of the irrepressible late fire chief. It was time for me to chat with relatives whom I could barely place in memory, but I needed to pretend to recognize. I was flying solo now—there were no longer any Winterset blood relatives who could help me identify these figures from my deep past. ⌘

# Postscript 3:
# The Small Town as an American Icon

There is a mysterious sense in which most Americans are small town products, no matter where they grew up.

When Europeans discovered America she had no cities. She had people, but they kept moving for the most part; nomads following the game supply or looking for fresh areas to forage for nature's bounty (or to escape nature's caprice). If they stayed put for long it was in small clusters, and without permanent structures. Maybe dwelling in permanent structures nature had provided, caves for example, but not building cities by constructing their own permanent structures.

Arriving Europeans, mostly rural folks anyway, either spread out on the agricultural landscape or gathered in small villages evoking the little patches of quasi-urbanity they knew from home. There would eventually be cities, but they would grow slowly. There was time to watch, and to understand that they grew from the solid foundations of very small towns.

Our American cities were not originally a given. We might have succeeded in building just a nation of farmers and small towns. That was most likely what the first European Americans expected, at least when they took the luxury of taking enough time out to even muse on such things. We watched the cities grow from the tiny seeds of villages, almost by accident as we attended to life's more pressing realities. And then we left a portion of our hearts back in those seedling gathering spots.

When American cities did arrive, they naturally became beacons for grand scale cooperation—showcases of art and industry, expressions and celebrations of society's catholicity. But small towns had already staked their claim on the American psyche. They had already staked their claim on America's soul—they were, and would remain, the centers of our virtue. Small town America encapsulated our innocence and our purpose.

Yes, we were becoming increasingly fascinated by the macro. But Americans had learned through hard work and a pioneer history to keep their feet on the ground. They tapped into their inner wisdom not to abandon the micro. It was a treasure to be preserved; a teacher to be heeded. Amidst all the cacophony of our adolescent spurt of growth, we somehow always knew where we were anchored.

The small town is embedded in our folklore and our dreams—in our basic identity. It's part of the structure and foundation of the American imagination. It's an American icon of life the way we're sure it's supposed to be lived. It's apple pie, it's Mother's apron strings, it's the watchfulness of a neighbor sitting on her front porch keeping a parental eye on neighborhood kids playing. It's working for an honest day's living and the pride which comes from the illusion of self-sufficiency.

Small town life is contributing to a common wealth. It touches all of us—even those who have only driven through one of these small towns while thinking, "Thank God I wasn't stuck here growing up." But in the back of their minds there was an unarticulated thought—a quick stab of envy for those who did experience the calm, the simplicity, the neighborliness, the innocence of this backbone of American life. We knew in our hearts that to find our country's 'salt of the earth' figures, one looked first in our small towns.

American values are small town values. We strive to live in harmony with each other and to give our neighbor the deference he deserves. These goals may have become greatly more difficult with time and may even seem out of reach in today's ultra-politicized society, but they are still what we hope for; they are still the ideal. We want safe, happy places for our kids to grow up. We want to feel that we belong, that we are rooted. We'll even sacrifice for the good of others, neighbors, when necessary.

The images evoked by our residential communities continue to feed the stereotypes. Someone says "political corruption, Mafia, crime" and the average Joe thinks "cities." Someone says "Grandma putting up preserves, back yard barbeque, high school prom" and the same guy thinks "small town" (or suburb, at worst). These images are baked into the American experience in general, even if we haven't experienced them as particular individuals.

Thornton Wilder is one of our great American iconographers, setting down the elements each of us carry in our hearts about our hometown. For some of us that hometown is, in fact, a small town. For others it is the *idea* of a small town; the closeness, the mutual caring, the mutual striving, the mutual shelter from life's harsher moments. Our small hometown does not have to be Grover's Corners—it does not even have to be Winterset. For some it may be a little section of a ghetto in a big city. But for all it is somehow Americana.

It's the innocence of heart which America cherishes, whether learned and practiced in an actual small town, or just inspired by the "Winterset" we all somehow instinctively know from our dreams—from just being Americans. America's small towns kept our feet on the ground. Everyone knew everyone else, including their foibles. It's more difficult to believe one is superior to a neighbor when the neighbor actually lives next door, literally or figuratively.

## Winterset In Time

In America the small town which is one's hometown does not have to be a specific place. It can be an idea, a vision, even just a hope. It is the place we know we belong even if we leave. The place where we have standing. We were simply too close to each other, in our small towns, to betray each other. As our towns grew into cities, we grew further apart from each other. The *idea* of the small town remained, however, growing more valuable, more cherished, and more patriotic as our cities grew.

There are those who seem to enjoy pointing out the difficulties and short comings of small town life. They may even label America's small town mythology a lie. But that ignores the fact that our small town folklore is not history, but an idea, and an ideal—an ideal to strive for rather than a past to live up to. Small town America is more an aspiration than nostalgia. And as such it is also a challenge. A challenge to keep our better angels in command; to live up to the American standard of decency which we all feel should rule, even if we have slightly different ideas of what the fine points of that standard consists of.

To walk in the sun through the heart of an American small town is to relax into the basic goodness of one's fellow humans. One feels safe because one intuits that the intentions of those passing by are just as innocent and generous as are one's own. I've lived in cities where people try not to engage the eyes of strangers. Not so in small towns, however. Walking the main street of an American small town is an exercise in openness and shared humanity. If one catches the eye of another person, he does not hurry away fearing he's just encountered a dangerous psychopath. He just smiles back at you. And he means the good will his smile signaled.

So my paean to Winterset is a paean to America and its plethora of Springfields and its treasury of Podunks. May we never lose our innocent striving. May we never lose the entrepreneurial spirit of our ancestors. May we never lose our reverence for the neighbor. We must never let our American small town values turn into a mere string of clichés. In our hearts we need always to keep one foot in Grover's Corners, or Mayberry, or better yet, in Winterset. ⌘

Made in the USA
Columbia, SC
18 August 2023